girl,
trans-
cending

girl, transcending

AJ CLEMENTINE

murdoch books

Sydney | London

To the angels and dreamers,
the resourceful and kind.

You are not weak.
Crying is strength and
imagination is power.

transcend

verb (t)

1. To go or be above or beyond
(a limit, something with limits, etc.);
surpass or exceed.

2. To go beyond in elevation,
excellence, extent, degree, etc.;
surpass, excel or exceed.

CONTENTS

Once upon a time...

...THERE WAS A LITTLE GIRL WITH A BIG
IMAGINATION, WARM HEART AND A BRIGHT
SPIRIT. SHE WAS SPECIAL BECAUSE SHE'D
BEEN BORN INSIDE A MAGICAL SHELL THAT
LOOKED LIKE A PERFECT LITTLE BOY. SHE
DREAMED OF ONE DAY FINDING A MAGIC MIRROR
THAT WOULD REVEAL HER TRUE SELF — THE
LITTLE GIRL SHE KNEW HERSELF TO BE.

WITHIN THE WALLS OF HER FAMILY'S HOME,
SHE WAS SAFE AND LOVED. SHE'D PUT ON
HER PRETTY CLOTHES AND DANCE AROUND,
AND THE LIGHT INSIDE HER WOULD GLOW.
BUT OUTSIDE THOSE WALLS, THE WORLD WAS
DARK AND CONFUSING. WHEN SHE WAS OUT
THERE, SHE'D PRETEND TO BE THAT LITTLE
BOY BECAUSE THAT'S WHAT SHE BELIEVED
THE WORLD WANTED HER TO BE.

AS THE YEARS WENT ON, HER SHELL BECAME
HEAVIER AND HARDER TO CARRY. AND IT
GREW DARKER AND COLDER INSIDE IT. THE
GIRL TRIED TO STAY HOPEFUL, BUT THAT
LONGED-FOR MAGIC MIRROR WAS NOWHERE TO
BE FOUND. SHE THOUGHT SHE MIGHT HAVE
TO WEAR THE SHELL FOREVER — IT SEEMED
EASIER THAN TRYING TO FIND A WAY TO TAKE
IT OFF. BUT THE LIGHT INSIDE HER WAS
RESTLESS AND BEGAN TO BURN TINY HOLES
THROUGH THE SHELL, UNTIL EVENTUALLY,
PEOPLE STARTED TO SEE HOT WHITE
PINPRICKS OF LIGHT SHINING THROUGH.

THE PEOPLE WHO LOVED HER HELD HER HAND AS
HER LIGHT BURNED AWAY THE THICK, BRITTLE
SHELL FROM THE INSIDE OUT. AND WHEN THE
LAST PIECES OF THE SHELL FINALLY FELL
AWAY, SHE STEPPED OUT INTO THE WORLD —
REALISING THERE WAS NO MAGIC MIRROR,
THERE HAD ONLY EVER BEEN HER OWN COURAGE,
WILLING HER TO BLOSSOM AND REVEAL THE
WOMAN SHE WAS DESTINED TO BE.

WHEN the LAST PiECES of the SHELL FiNALLY FELL AWAY, SHE STEPPED out into the WorLd

Welcome to my story – it's not a guide to transitioning or growing into who you're meant to be. It's more of a behind-the-scenes look at how I got through the best and worst parts of my life. It's about how I learned to fall in love with 'someday soons' and a 'your time will come' mentality – two things that pulled me through a lot of hard times.

I talk freely and am open about my transition and my personal experiences in public and in this book so that other people who need to can hopefully take something from them. I don't speak for all trans people – how it is for me isn't how it may be for the next girl or the next guy. It's so important that people understand that just because I talk about my life on this intimate level, it doesn't mean another trans person will want to do the same. This is a personal and private journey, and nobody owes anyone their story, which is why in this book I've changed some people's names to protect their privacy.

EDUCATING OURSELVES ABOUT SOMEONE ELSE'S EXPERIENCE IS THE BEST WAY TO CREATE MORE EMPATHY IN THE WORLD

If you aren't trans, but you have questions about some aspect of the trans experience, it's okay to be curious. I learn new things from people I follow all the time. Educating ourselves about someone else's experience is the best way to create more empathy and understanding in the world. The trick is satisfying that curiosity in a respectful way. All the information you could ever need is on YouTube

TRANS PEOPLE DON'T
EXIST TO ENTERTAIN
PEOPLE'S CURIOSITY

these days, so start there. Watch my videos, watch videos from other trans creators, read more books like this one, follow trans activists on social media. But please don't ask a trans person invasive questions about their body, just because *you* want to know. Trans people don't exist to entertain or amuse anyone. There's a difference between respectful curiosity and straight-up rude. If you aren't sure if your question crosses that line, here's an easy check: would you ask a cisgender person you didn't know the same thing?

I hope that sharing my experiences and some of the things that have helped me might help you, too, regardless of what sort of shell you might be carrying. We live so much of our lives online these days that it becomes our highlight reel. It can be hard to convey the harder moments that make up so much of our lives. This book is about those parts – the ones you don't see.

Sometimes you can't have the best without experiencing the worst.

'Mum?'

—— 'Yes?'

'Did God make me this way because
he doesn't like me?'

—— 'You're exactly the way you're
supposed to be. It's not a mistake.'

Like most little girls, I wanted to be just like my mum when I grew
up, and I assumed I would be. I thought she was beautiful and so
strong, and she had this self-assurance that whatever she was doing
was the right thing. If other people disagreed, it was because *they*
were wrong. That even applied to religion. Mum grew up Catholic,
and although religion was important to her, she didn't go in for all of
the strict rules. Instead, she raised us to believe that being a good
person was the only thing that *really* mattered.

My perception of the world from inside my own little bubble
was that it was a vibrant and happy place – somewhere filled with
possibilities and good people. But the more time I spent in the real
world with my mum, the more that vision started to crumble. In
supermarkets, post offices, restaurants and train stations, I'd stand
by Mum's side as strangers mimicked her in broken English or spoke

Mum
x

to her EXTRA slow, like they were talking to someone from another planet. Alarm bells would ring inside my head and I'd think, *Wait, why are they speaking to her like that? I can understand her. I know what she's saying, and she understands me. So why are they treating her as someone who isn't like me or like them?*

People talked down to her.

People cut in front of her in queues, like she wasn't even there.

Old men would try to flirt with her, or degrade her by saying nasty things under their breath.

I'm sure there was so much more I didn't see.

One day, a lady in the supermarket said something racist to Mum, and my hot-headed mother rammed her trolley right into that woman's cart. I still don't know what that woman said to make her do that; I just remember feeling so confused. My mum was a proud Filipina and the kindest person I knew. What could she possibly be doing to make strangers treat her this way? None of it made any sense to me.

My child's mind may not have understood race or racism, but it was starting to grasp that people weren't always who I thought they were, and that scared me. I was too young to see that there were 'rules' or set ways to raise a child just because of how they were born. At home, Mum let me wear the dresses I loved, play with her makeup and do all of the things that made me feel like myself. And when I'd take my dolls out of the house with me, she wouldn't stop me, but she would gently try to explain that the world might not understand me. She'd say, 'People will think this is weird, because little boys aren't supposed to play with these types of toys.' But my happiness was always more important to her than the approval of strangers, so she never forced me to conform.

The older I got, the more I understood that Mum was trying to protect me from what she was already experiencing. She didn't look or sound 'Australian enough', and that made it hard for her to fit into Australian culture. I was half Filipino and half white, so my heritage wasn't as obvious as hers. The target on my back was there for a different reason: because the things I naturally gravitated to were 'girl' things. Around the age of seven, I went into self-protection mode and thought, *Okay, I need to find ways to blend in with the rest of the kids*. I started playing a boy's sport and demonstrating more 'masculine' interests when I was out in the world. It wasn't healthy for me, but I found ways to cope.

My main coping strategy was to exist inside my daydreams. I didn't like what I was seeing around me – I wanted to be someone else, somewhere else. If I could live my life within my head, then I figured that would get me through until the day I developed into a woman. I didn't know anything about puberty yet – I just assumed I'd grow into the woman I was destined to be. And I comforted myself by thinking, *One day soon, I'll get to truly be myself. But right now, I have to play this role of being a little boy who likes feminine things.*

IF YOU FEEL LIKE YOUR TIME IS NEVER GOING TO COME, DON'T GIVE UP. YOUR TIME WILL COME – IT WILL.

As a kid, I held on to those 'someday soons', and I think that's why I'm able to look back now and say I had a pretty good childhood. In my imagination, the alternate reality I created for myself was so vivid, and felt so real to me, that I got comfort from living in that world. And because of that, I was able to find peace in different parts of my life. I believed there were good things to look forward to, even if I hadn't experienced them yet. I fell in love with fictional characters and held on to the belief that I'd find people like them in my real life. Now that I've spoken about this on social media, I've had a lot of people reach out to tell me that they do the same thing. It's how they deal with their own trauma.

my 'someday soons' kept me going

The outside world was confusing and scary to me, but when I was at home, I was safe. I had my dolls, my Barbies, my clothes, and all the other things that made me feel like *me*. I knew I couldn't bring those things into real life, but that was fine for that moment. I knew my time would come.

If you feel like your time is never going to come, don't give up. Your time will come – it will.

it's a girl!

When people ask how I came out to my parents, I tell them I didn't have to. It was always *known* that I was a girl – it's just that none of us knew how to put that into words.

I grew up with my mum, stepdad and older brother, Dane – and later, my younger half-siblings Kiana (aka Kiki) and Sean. My biological dad lives interstate with my stepmother and half-sister, Kali. Even though Dane and I would stay with my biological dad every holiday, my stepdad was always 'Dad' to me. In Mum and Dad's house, I was free to be who I was.

I was probably around five when I started noticing that people weren't as accepting of me as my parents were. Little situations here and there would bring their true feelings out – like when my biological dad got together with my stepmother. She was really nice at first, but when I'd go to stay with them and my biological dad and Dane weren't around, it became clear that she didn't like me looking at her perfumes or make-up, or playing with Kali's girly toys. She'd take those things away from me and refuse to let me have them, which was so confusing, because all I'd ever known was that being inside a house meant being safe and being free to be myself. I couldn't understand why the rules were suddenly changing.

When I told Mum what was happening, she confronted my biological dad. He defended his then-girlfriend and said he didn't feel that she was doing anything wrong. He said maybe it was my mum's fault for encouraging my behaviour. In hindsight, I think the

Left: Me and my *kuya* (older brother), Dane.
Below left: My stepdad (aka Dad) holding me.
Below: I was obsessed with this car seat!

I WAS PROBABLY AROUND FIVE WHEN I STARTED NOTICING THAT PEOPLE WEREN'T AS ACCEPTING OF ME AS MY PARENTS WERE

if only we'd known

Cisgender (or cis) people identify with being the same gender as their biological sex. Transgender people identify with being the opposite gender to their biological sex. Until recently, there wasn't a lot of research done into transgenderism, so it was very misunderstood – even by the scientific world. But recent studies have shown that trans brains behave like the brains of the gender they desire to be from an early age. So, a trans boy's brain may display more activity in the parts of the brain that govern spatial awareness – resembling the brain of a cis boy.

'Gender incongruence' is where a person's sense of identity doesn't match their physical body, and it often triggers a condition known as 'gender dysphoria', which is the distress caused by feeling like you're in the wrong body. Gender dysphoria can show up in early childhood and cause a lot of psychological distress, especially if you don't know what it is, or how to treat it – which is how it went down for me and my family.

Dr Julie Bakker, who led a 2018 study into the brains of trans teens, suggests that earlier diagnosis or better understanding of transgenderism could help to improve quality of life for young transgender people, and help families make more informed decisions on treatment. That's what it's all about.

way he and my stepmother felt about me preferring 'girl's' toys was probably typical of their generation. Both of them grew up seeing such strongly defined gender roles around them that they couldn't accept that some people don't fit neatly into those boxes. They didn't understand it or know what to do with it.

At the time, I wasn't able to say, 'I'M ACTUALLY A GIRL!', because I didn't have the knowledge to put my feelings into words. And the adults around me didn't have the resources or tools to understand what was going on with me, either. It was confusing – for all of us. In the end, I stopped visiting my biological dad, and it stayed that way for the rest of my childhood.

I WASN'T ABLE TO SAY, 'I'M ACTUALLY A GIRL!', BECAUSE I DIDN'T HAVE THE KNOWLEDGE TO PUT MY FEELINGS INTO WORDS

My older brother, Dane, continued to have a great relationship with our biological dad, and as we got older, he always reminded me that my biological dad cared for me, too. Deep down, I knew there was love, but I had too many of my own struggles to deal with first. Having to visit my biological dad and stay somewhere I didn't feel free to be myself was too much, so I put my relationship with him and Kali on hold until I could figure out who I was.

Throughout our childhood, my brother Dane took on the role of my protector. I think he was scared of what people might say or do to me. Even though his high school was really far away, he'd walk me to school first, and if someone was bullying me, he'd wait for me outside school so he could walk me home. But he also struggled with me playing with dolls. Although he never tried to stop me, he'd say, 'It's okay to play with them, just don't play with them around me.' I could tell he was secretly ashamed of my toys, but I never got WHY it was so bad.

The older I got, the more the judgement and disapproval from other people started to get to me. I went from being this confident kid who would take my dolls everywhere, and didn't care what people thought, to being so much more reserved and guarded. But Mum continued to see me for who I really was. And she would always reassure me that it would all make sense one day, because she believed it would. Having her acceptance was so important; it was something to cling to when everyone else was sending me the message that what I was doing was wrong.

CHILDREN SHOULDN'T FEEL THAT THEY NEED TO BLEND IN, OR BE MADE TO FEEL THERE'S SOMETHING WRONG WITH THEM

Mum really struggled to know if she was doing the right thing. People were telling her she was wrong for buying me certain toys, or for letting me dress in the clothes I preferred. Everyone was against her, including my biological dad, and I could see that. Back then, she didn't know how to use the internet, and wouldn't have had the first clue what to search for. She was parenting from pure instinct, and going off what her friends told her. All she wanted to do was make

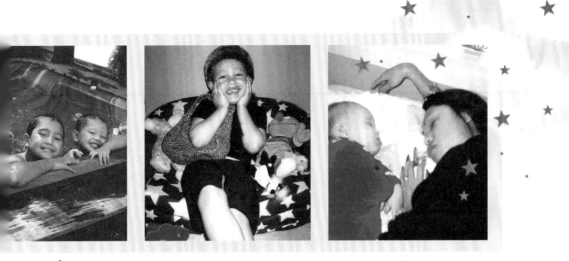

Left: Dane and me splashing around. Middle: Mum let me into her wardrobe so I could dress up for a photo shoot. Right: Dad noticed early on that Mum and I have the same sleeping face.

my brother, the protector!

me happy, but I saw the judgement all around us, so I did what I could to try to blend in.

What I understand now is that children shouldn't feel that they need to blend in, or be made to feel there's something wrong with them. We should be creating environments where kids feel that they're okay exactly as they are, and giving them safe spaces to grow into themselves without fear.

Obviously, kids need to know that the world isn't always sunshine and rainbows. But they shouldn't be told that what *they're* doing is bad, or that *their* interests and likes are going to define their whole being. Toys and clothes aren't linked to gender, but I think people get that confused. It's true that I liked dolls and dresses, but they weren't part of me. Even if I'd played with trucks and water guns (which I did, by the way), I would still have been a girl at the end of the day.

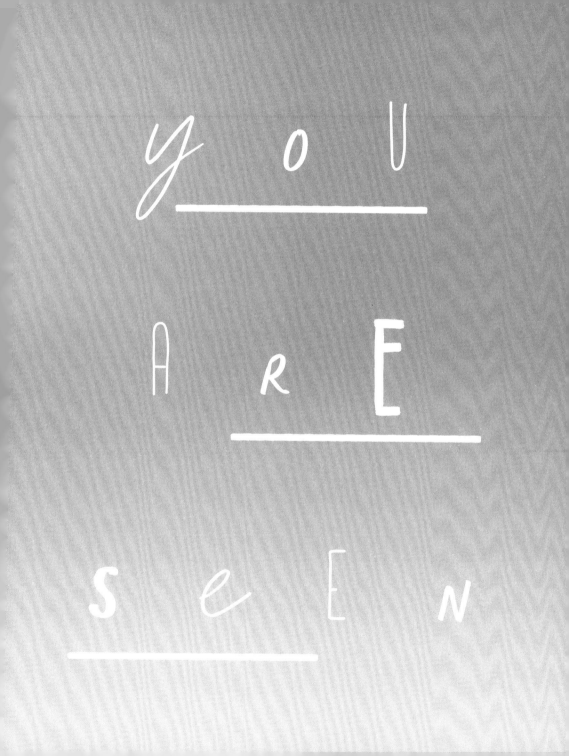

living my dream!

RiGHT NOW, in this moment,

I'm living the life I dreamed about when I was that little kid existing in my daydream.

Actually, it's even better than I imagined. I'm true to myself and I'm putting that energy back into the world. When people look at me, they see the person I've always known I was, and the people I'm close to and choose to spend my time with validate me and see me for who I really am.

But how I feel today is definitely not how I always felt. It took time to get here, and a lot of that time wasn't easy. So if you don't feel seen right now, or if you feel like giving up on yourself, please know that there ARE people out there who will hold you up and care for you – you just haven't met them yet. Hold on, bby!

While you're waiting for those special people to come into your life, explore ways to validate yourself. Some people look for comfort in alcohol or drugs, but there are much less toxic ways to get to the same place. Somehow, through simple objects and fantasies, I was able to stay positive. Rather than get mad at the world or lash out, I found my own ways to get through tough times; I just felt there was a way to get what I wanted that didn't involve anger.

Over the next few pages, I'm going to share some of the objects, people and moments that meant something to me and pulled me through. I still lean on some of them in my adult life – they're there for me when I need them.

toddle and tot

I loved a lot of toys when I was little, but I was super obsessed with Beanie Kids, which come in a whole range of different personalities with their own outfits. The female characters – nurses, fairytale characters, mermaids – were my favourites, but the ones I loved most of all were the boy and girl twins called Toddle and Tot. I'd create worlds with them and just live in that daydream. They were such an escape for me. What is it that makes you feel like yourself? Art? Music? Acting? Throw yourself into that thing and let it fill you up, and keep you connected to who you are.

lip gloss and the wild youth

When I was in primary school, one of my teenage cousins was going through a rebellious stage at home. Her parents sent her to live with us, and when she moved into our house with all of her teen girl energy and her teen girl things, I was in awe of her. Walking into her bedroom and seeing her stuff everywhere was so inspiring – she was everything I wanted to be. She had this jar of lip glosses sitting on the dresser in her bedroom, and each morning, I'd go into her room without asking and take a different lip gloss. And just for that day, I'd use it in secret.

THOSE LIP GLOSSES SYMBOLISED EVERYTHING I WANTED TO BE

I'd keep that lip gloss in my pocket all day at school, and even though I wouldn't show it to anyone else, I knew it was there, and it was adding to who I truly was inside. During this confusing time in my life, just holding on to a simple tube of her lip gloss empowered me in some way. It was as if part of me was living a fantasy, because she was a teenage girl, and that's what I wanted to be more than anything. I didn't know how it would happen, but I knew this lip gloss was creating this future for me somehow. Even though I had short hair and people were calling me a little boy, I felt like, *It's okay, I have this lip gloss in my pocket. I know who I am. I don't care what other people think or say.*

It's wild how we can latch on to certain objects like this – and how the simplest things can mean the most. Those lip glosses symbolised everything I wanted to be, and somehow my cousin saw that. Eventually, she found out that I was taking them, but she never said anything. And when she moved back home, she gave me that whole jar of lip glosses to keep, as her parting gift to me. She knew how much I liked and needed them. Somehow, they made me feel like I could take on the world – like I was going to be able to get what I needed one day.

And to this day, your girl loves a glossy lip!

IT'S WILD HOW WE CAN LATCH ON TO OBJECTS LIKE THIS - AND HOW THE SIMPLEST THINGS CAN MEAN THE MOST

still love my gloss! →

Above: Rapunzel vibes.
Left: A visit to Mum's closet turns into a runway show.

the state of dreaming

The ability to make up a game in the moment was something I had from early on. I was always the one people would turn to when we needed an idea. One of my best childhood friends, Riya, really loved my games, and she never questioned my toys or made me feel bad for having them. Our friendship was special to me. She would often get bullied for being Indian, and where I was able to 'blend in' and hide my Asian heritage most of the time, Riya couldn't deny hers – and she didn't want to. I was so impressed by the way she would stand up to the bullies and take pride in herself.

But then, right before we started high school, Riya disappeared. I was devastated because I didn't know where she'd gone. I thought that she didn't want our friendship anymore. Shortly after that, my family moved to another suburb, making it even harder for us to find each other. When we reconnected recently, she explained that she'd gone to India for high school because she'd struggled to fit in with Australian culture. Turned out Indian culture wasn't an easy fit, either.

bubble tea sister date

YOU ALWAYS GRAVITATE TO PEOPLE WHO MAKE YOU FEEL VALIDATED IN THAT MOMENT

Reconnecting with Riya made me realise how much we both used those childhood games as an escape from how people were treating us. We were both different in a world where people didn't understand us, but we understood each other. Riya wasn't surprised to hear what I'm doing these days; it made sense to her.

Childhood friendships say a lot about your character as you move into adulthood. You always gravitate to people who make you feel validated in that moment, and even if those people aren't destined to be in your future, their impact never leaves you.

Opposite page, from left: Celebrating Trans Visibility Day with my fairy bestie, Bambi; commuting to a photo shoot; me and Kiki getting our fave taro bubble tea in 2020. Below, from left: Soaking up the sun next to some train tracks; a yellow bandaid was a prop for a TikTok moment; in Sydney with Ryan – our first trip together.

standing with an army

In Year 2, my mum took me and my brother out of school for eight months, and we flew to the Philippines with her. When we came back, Riya and I were still best friends, but because I had to start Year 2 afresh, she was now a year above me. There was a shift in the friendship group, and I ended up becoming close with a group of girls in my year. They were known as the popular girls, but it wasn't a *Mean Girls* type of situation – everyone was really sweet and we all got along so well. I loved being part of this group.

Ava was everyone's favourite. She was so pretty: blonde hair, blue eyes – the definition of the Western beauty standard. I was closest to her because I wanted to BE her. And then there was Sophia, who'd always stick up for me when I was expressing more feminine attributes. I always felt safe around her, and with that whole group – like I could do anything. It was a happy time for me. When you have personalities that sync with each other, gender doesn't come into it. Or at least, it shouldn't . . .

I guess seeing a young boy be part of such a tight-knit girl group must have bothered the adults, because midway through the school year, the teachers started pulling my friends aside and telling them to distance themselves from me, so I had a chance to make friends with boys instead. That was the very last thing I wanted to do, but it didn't feel like I was being given a choice.

WHEN YOU HAVE PERSONALITIES THAT SYNC WITH EACH OTHER,

GENDER DOESN'T COME INTO IT

let's talk about schools

School (and life in general) would have been easier and less confusing for me if the adults around me had been better informed about trans issues. Maybe someone would have seen the signs that I was actually a little girl, and have been able to guide me and my parents to resources that could help us. Thankfully, things are changing, and the education system is doing more work to make schools safer and more inclusive for LGBTQ+ kids. That can only be a good thing, for all of us. I like to believe it will keep getting easier for kids to be themselves – but all of us need to stay on top of the people in power, and make sure we demand that they do better.

The Rainbow Owl (therainbowowl.com) has a list of resources for trans and gender diverse kids and their parents, as well as for educators and mental health professionals. And many places also have guidelines for schools posted online.

I've also been noticing that there are lots more children's books with trans or LGBTQ+ characters in them, and I'm so here for that. *My Shadow Is Pink* by Scott Stuart is a good story that puts into words how some children may feel. If ONLY I'd had a book like this when I was a child.

books for little kids

Paul Emerich France – an educational consultant in the US – wrote a great article about how to create an LGBTQ-inclusive classroom. His suggested reading list for ages 5–11 is below.

♥ *All Are Welcome* by Alexandra Penfold and Suzanne Kaufman

♥ *Julián Is a Mermaid* by Jessica Love

♥ *Pride: The Story of Harvey Milk and the Rainbow Flag* by Rob Sanders

♥ *Queer Heroes: Meet 52 LGBTQ Heroes from the Past and Present* by Arabelle Sicardi

♥ *Pink Is for Boys* by Robb Pearlman

♥ *A Family Is a Family Is a Family* by Sara O'Leary

♥ *George* by Alex Gino

♥ *The Boy and the Bindi* by Vivek Shraya

Another book I really love is:

♥ *My Shadow Is Pink* by Scott Stuart

Source: edutopia.org/article/supporting-lgbtq-students-elementary-school

metamorphosis

I was eight when I made my first best friend who was a boy. My girl group was slowly pulling away from me thanks to the teacher intervention, and this other kid and I just found ourselves gravitating to each other. Eventually, I willingly stopped playing with my girl group so I could play with this kid. I loved this new friendship so much. We had a lot in common, and I'd never had this type of connection with a boy. It was exciting.

At the time we became friends, our classes were taking swimming lessons, and the boys had to get changed in a communal change room. I remember how this made both of us really uncomfortable. We didn't like that the adults or other boys could see us – actually, we hated it. So we'd shield each other while getting changed. It felt so good to have someone in that room who not only understood how I felt, but also felt the same.

We stayed friends for a couple of months but then, suddenly, something changed. They turned up at school one day and said they didn't want to be friends anymore. They said the friendship had just been a temporary thing, and that we weren't really friends. I was crushed. What had forced this sudden change? I remember thinking, *I've tried my best. Why can't I just fit in? Why is it so difficult?*

Up until a year ago – into my twenties – the sudden ending of this friendship still confused me. But then I got a DM with a last name I recognised, and it was them. Turns out they are trans, too.

And you know what?

I wasn't even shocked because I *understood* it.

Her message was very sweet. She apologised for letting go of the friendship and explained that, at that time in her life, it was too much of feeling the same. This revelation was so interesting because it meant that the one time in my life I *thought* I'd connected and made friends with a boy, I'd actually made friends with another girl. (What are the odds!)

NEITHER OF US HAD THE INFORMATION WE NEEDED TO EXPLAIN WHAT WAS HAPPENING IN OUR MINDS AND BODIES

But it makes sense. As two confused kids, we'd related on so many levels – we just hadn't known how to put our feelings into words. And because I was that little bit more comfortable in my skin back then, and more connected to knowing that I was going to be a girl one day (even if I didn't know HOW), it was too overwhelming for her because being friends with me was forcing her to confront what she wanted out of life. But, like me, she was trapped in a transphobic way of thinking: *This is wrong, I should be trying to blend in.*

Neither of us had the information we needed to explain what was happening in our minds and bodies, or a roadmap to guide us through feelings and questions way above our maturity level. And that took a toll on both of us. So many adults go their whole lives without having a good grasp of their identity, or knowing who they truly are. How are children supposed to know how to navigate that?

pronouns matter

In the story I just shared, I introduced my 'new best friend' as a 'boy'. But that was purely to illustrate how, in my child's mind, I believed I was forming a friendship with a boy in that moment. Turns out I wasn't. She was always a girl; she just presented as a little boy at that time. Same as me.

Many cisgender people, especially older generations, don't get why pronouns mean so much to people in the LGBTQ+ community, or why these little words hold so much power – but they DO hold power. Let's take a trans woman, for example. Cisgender people who refuse to accept her as a woman will show their disapproval and hate by using male pronouns to refer to her. Not only is that incorrect and disrespectful, but it can also cause trauma by triggering that person's dysphoria.

Even if cis people do accept her for who she is, and use the correct pronouns for her in the present moment, many will still make the mistake of misgendering her when referring to her past. People like to draw a line across the timeline of a trans person's life and see them as one gender before their transition, and another gender after the point of transition. It's neat and tidy for them that way. But just because the world saw that woman as male for a period of her life doesn't mean she wasn't a girl the whole time. In her brain, in her heart, she was always a woman. Referring to her with male pronouns in the past tense still invalidates her true identity. She has been a 'she' the whole timeline of her life, even if the world didn't see her that way.

There is a person in my own extended family who continues to misgender me to this day, and it hurts. No matter how many times other family members correct this person and explain why what they're saying is hurtful and wrong, they insist on doing it. And because of that, I try to avoid contact with that person as much as I can. When they look at me, I know they see me as a little boy – they just can't let that go. This triggers my dysphoria and has the power to ruin my day, so I stay away.

My parents try their best, but occasionally they'll slip up and refer to me as 'he' when recalling my childhood. I remind them that those pronouns don't make sense. I was still me – still female then. It's even worse when parents treat their trans child's transition as a death. It's hard enough for a young person to go through their transition, let alone go through it feeling like they've 'killed' their parents' son or daughter. That's so intense! It makes the situation more dramatic than it needs to be. Their child is still right there; it's so hurtful to suggest otherwise.

wild world

Around the same time that new friendship ended, I turned to a game for comfort again, only this time it wasn't one I made up. It was Animal Crossing, which I had on Nintendo DS. It was very new at the time, and it brought me so much joy you don't even know!

It was this simple world where your villager completes day-to-day tasks. The game works in real time, too, so if you start building a bridge, you have to check back later to see if that bridge has been built. The characters in the game have personalities and interact with each other in a really sweet way. My villager was female (of course!) and I dressed her in the clothes I wanted to wear in real life. She went shopping, fishing, made mortgage payments, spent days pulling weeds . . . I felt so free playing that game. It was this secret, safe place waiting for me after school. It gave me hope.

finding a safe online place to play gave me hope

For a while, I honestly thought I was the only person playing this game, but then I found other people who loved it, too, and we started playing together, which was so much fun. I loved that the game didn't ask much of me. It was simple, and that's what I wanted life to be. I wanted to live in that game and be that character, and not have to think about so many confusing adult things. That game is what it should be like to be young. Kids should be able to just be in the moment and live life.

In the years since then, I've been on forums and read so many stories about how Animal Crossing helped other people through tough times. Even if you don't have friends in real life in that moment, at least you have the animals in the game, with different personalities. They're relying on you to return to the game, and there's something comforting about that. Sometimes, you just need that bridge to get you from one phase of life to another.

> **I FELT SO FREE PLAYING THAT GAME.
> IT WAS THIS SECRET, SAFE PLACE**

mother knows best

When Mum was growing up in the Philippines, it was a very traditional and conservative country, with a big Catholic population. For the most part, people stuck to their religious values and views, but even though she was religious, Mum never subscribed to most of the rules and restrictions of her religion. She sticks to what she believes in, and does what she feels is right. At her core, she believes that if you're kind and a good person, that's all that really matters.

Trans people are still not part of mainstream culture in the Philippines. Of course, there are trans people in that country, but they aren't accepted as such. The only thing Mum knew of in Filipino culture was a *bakla*, a Tagalong term describing a man who prefers feminine gender expression or identifies as a woman. This umbrella term covers everything from being effeminate to cross-dressing or being trans, and is more about gender expression than sexuality.

Love you, mama!

When I was twelve, Mum took me to see a few drag queen shows on one of our trips to the Philippines. She thought maybe that was the answer for me – something I could do when I grew up. I loved the theatre of it! But for me, being a girl wasn't something I wanted to take off and put on like a costume. It wasn't for show – it was how I wanted to live life every day. I told Mum that it wasn't for me, and we moved on. But just knowing that she was searching for answers with me, even if we weren't finding the right ones, gave me confidence that I would get to where I needed to be one day.

how to save a life

Our search for answers continued into my early teens, when my naive expectation that I'd somehow grow into a woman were shattered once I learned the actual facts around puberty. The search would have gone on for even longer if it hadn't been for my high-school English teacher, who passed me a piece of paper that turned out to be a lightning bolt right through my life. During a quiet reading session, he passed me a short story he'd clipped from a newspaper. It was about this sixteen-year-old German girl, Kim Petras, who was transgender and had just become the youngest person in the world to have gender confirmation surgery. The way the article was written made it sound like these surgeries had been happening in Germany for a long time. My mind couldn't even comprehend that this was a thing. I thought, *Wait, is this something I could have one day? How?*

IF PEOPLE WERE BORN IN THE WRONG BODY, THEY COULD JUST TRANSITION!

The second I got home from school, I went online and found all this information about trans people and transitioning, and how this was normalised in Germany and not something taboo – or at least not as taboo as it seemed to be in Australia. If people in Germany were born in the wrong body, they could just transition! WHAT! I shared this information with my mum and it started to make sense to her.

After years of confusion, this teacher had handed me a word to explain my experience: trans. Learning about Kim and her surgery didn't mean I was ready to embrace being a trans person yet, or put that label on myself – far from it. But it was the first piece of the puzzle.

I don't know whether my teacher was in the LGBTQ+ community or just an ally, but I do know that I really needed the information he gave me in that moment.

kiki, I adore you!

my light bulb moment

A lot of stuff changed when my little sister Kiana (Kiki) was born. I was nine at the time, and as I watched the world give her all the things I had to fight to have, I couldn't help feeling envious and jealous of her. But as she got older, I realised it wasn't her fault. She hadn't asked to play that role in my life, and she wasn't there to make me feel jealous of her 24/7. The fact that she was a trigger to me had nothing to do with her – it was all on me. I had to realise that if I didn't work though those feelings and deal with them, we'd always have that tension.

Slowly, envy turned into a deep connection. I had a friend in her, even though she was so young. Kiki never saw gender at all – she was so easy and accepting of me. I think kids have the capacity to understand and accept so quickly compared with adults, and that's beautiful in itself.

Almost the same personality on the Myer Briggs scale, only I'm the introverted version and she's the extroverted one.

Raised her to be my twin. We love serving the same lewk.

Kiki

Just by being the little girl she was, Kiki reminded me of the things I'd liked as a kid, and the things I was leaving behind as I was growing into a teen. She helped me reconnect with parts of my childhood, and she made me feel seen, especially during my late teens when I started to transition. Somehow, she was really aware and emotionally intelligent when it came to how I was feeling. When I started growing my hair out, she'd instinctively know when to come into my space, braid my hair and make it look cute, like I used to do for her when she was little.

Now that she's in high school, I'm constantly blown away by how informed and confident Kiki is. When I was her age, I'd close up and shrink from confronting situations. I was way too scared of drawing attention to myself. But more than that, I didn't feel I could speak up, because I didn't feel like a person. I was just drifting through life, hoping that one day I'd be happy and at peace with myself. That I'd be . . . a whole person. And Kiki's already there.

If she hears kids at her school using slurs or saying horrible things, she'll call them out on it and tell them why it's wrong. Playing this role is frustrating for her, though, and sometimes it upsets her. She'll say, 'I don't get why these kids don't want to be good people!'

It's not that they don't want to be good, I tell her, it's just that at this point in their life, they care more about being liked and being popular than doing the right thing. And all they see when you correct them is that you're trying to attack them. If you want to tell them the right thing, you've done your part, but don't take it to heart if they don't want to listen or if they keep doing it. They're doing it because

Top left: Me and Kiki trying out a filter.
Bottom left: Squeezing Kiki at Moomba Festival.
Right: New Year's Day 2021 with my faves, Bambi and Kiki.

they're a child. Hopefully, they'll grow up. And when they grow up, they'll reflect and think, *Wow, that wasn't great*.

Kiki came into my life at the exact right moment, and our connection is something I treasure. Even now, we match our outfits and get inspired by each other, and since moving into my own place, I miss having that shared space to enjoy those simple moments as sisters. But when a bond with someone is this deep, that energy is still there. That natural connection never goes away.

tea in wonderland

An Instagram account I created in high school,
with nearly 1000 followers.

Social media has been part of my journey for such a long time; in a
way, it's been really important to my growth and headspace. I put my
thoughts, interests, ideas and experiences out into the world – and
I get to respond to people when they have misconceptions or are
misinformed about trans or LGBTQ+ issues. There's something so
freeing about having these platforms, because I also feel validated
by people who reach out and let me know that they see me. I love
it when strangers share their experiences with me, or ask questions

respectfully, or ask for advice. And I love how people let me know that I'm lifting them up in some way. That was something I just didn't have as a kid, and maybe if I had, I would have understood myself more and struggled a little less. If I can be that for someone else – and make them feel seen when they're confused or alone or scared – how amazing is that?

In the early days, Tumblr was my go-to. It's where I found people to lift me up in my darkest times. I had music that would play on shuffle on my Tumblr page, and my playlist even caught the attention of the popular girls at school, who would tell me that they listened to it for their bath tunes.

People shared so much on Tumblr, and I was shown information I'd never been exposed to. I loved how I could interact with people from all walks of life, and learn so much about someone just from their Tumblr blog. In many ways, I feel like TikTok is the modern version of this – maybe that's why I feel so comfortable there. From Tumblr, I started my YouTube channel and blog, *Tea in Wonderland*, and grew a following really quickly. And because I was real about who I was, what I was going through and how my life was unfolding, they completely got who I was as a person. They still do.

IN THE EARLY DAYS, TUMBLR WAS MY GO-TO.
IT'S WHERE I FOUND PEOPLE TO LIFT ME UP
IN MY DARKEST TIMES

girl, you're a girl

Roxy was self-aware, open and secure in herself – all the things I wasn't (yet) – and we became friends when I was sixteen. She was more experienced than me in so many ways, and would talk about her sexuality openly. I admired that about her, but I was also envious of her, and found her openness confronting because I wasn't there yet. We had so many great moments together, but we'd also bicker and fight – mostly because of my jealousy.

Being Roxy's friend was special, though, because I felt like she *really* knew who I was. I'd wear wigs and makeup at our sleepovers and we'd have a great time together – there was no judgement. Ours was an intense friendship, and Roxy helped me realise a lot of things about myself. She saw things in me that I wasn't ready to see. One night, she looked at me and said, 'I've done a lot of research, and I think you might be trans.'

Silence

Since learning about Kim Petras the previous year, I'd decided that being trans wasn't for me. Internet searches of trans people had shown me Kim living her best life, yes, but also plenty of other stuff that wasn't so positive. I'd heard the term 'tranny' thrown around a few times, so of course I'd searched that word and all kinds of disgusting videos and images popped up. These days, if you search that word, it will tell you right away that it's a slur. But when I searched it as a teen, almost all of the results were related to porn – trans people were hypersexualised as fetishes. There was no way of relating to them on a human level.

Hollywood wasn't a friendly place, either. Everywhere I looked, trans people were the butt of jokes. One of the biggest movies of 2011, the year I turned fifteen, was *The Hangover, Part II*. In one scene, one of the main characters gets drunk and hooks up with a trans woman. When he finds out she's trans, his first reaction is to vomit. Imagine being a teenager and seeing that a person would vomit if they hooked up with someone like you. To me, Kim Petras was living in a different world – a world where it was easier for her to be a woman. I was just a kid dressing up at sleepovers. I felt so far behind Kim in the transition process that I couldn't see how I'd ever be able to transition and feel validated as a female.

The message seemed clear: being trans was NOT a good thing. This created a never-ending battle inside me: part of me feeling that I was trans, and the other part fighting it, because WHY would I want to be something the rest of the world was so disgusted by? By the time Roxy told me she thought I was trans, I had so much internalised transphobia that I couldn't even entertain the idea. Her words weren't intended to hurt me, but they did. First, I was shocked, and then I was so angry. My response to her was, 'How dare you say I'm that!'

Roxy had seen me. I just wasn't ready.

the prom queen

Thankfully, something eventually shifted in me. By the time I turned seventeen I'd made it through one of the darkest, lowest years of my life, and I'd also discovered Andreja Pejić, a transgender model from Melbourne! Suddenly, transitioning wasn't a fantasy taking place on the other side of the world, it was something people were doing in my own city. I thought, *Hang on, if this is really who I am, why am I living a lie? If Kim Petras and Andreja Pejić are the only trans women I see, but they don't reflect who I am, why don't I try to redefine what being trans can be? Why don't I try to create something that IS me?* I knew I wasn't going to survive in this world if I kept lying to myself.

SUDDENLY, TRANSITIONING WASN'T A FANTASY TAKING PLACE ACROSS THE WORLD

I started investigating my options, and found out that transitioning as a teen in Australia was pretty complicated. If you are high-school age, which I was at that time, you have to petition the courts to get the hormone blockers that stop puberty in its tracks. I knew if I brought this up with my mum, she'd go through with the court process to make me happy, but the idea of court felt too scary. I decided to wait until I was eighteen to start medically transitioning – after all, it was only a year away. Instead, I'd start to socially transition while I was waiting. When it came to puberty, I was a late bloomer anyway, so

I didn't have many masculine features. In fact, when I had my first hormone test, my doctor told me I had higher than average levels of oestrogen, so in that sense, I was pretty lucky.

these were some of the steps I took to transition socially ...

♥ I changed my wardrobe to embrace more feminine looks.

♥ I introduced a few makeup and beauty products into my daily look.

♥ I painted my nails (even though it got me in trouble at school).

♥ I wore a knot headband to school.

♥ I started growing my hair longer.

♥ I mapped out a game plan for my transition.

♥ I worked on accepting the 'trans' label a bit more.

Top: Trying out new looks.
Middle: Rooftop patio, Manila, Philippines, aged 19.
Bottom: Bathroom selfie on a family trip, aged 17.

I also stopped looking for comfort in food, started exercising and eating healthy foods. I didn't want to hide anymore. I knew kids in my school would question these changes, but they were ALREADY saying stuff about me anyway, so I adopted a 'fuck it' mentality. Every day in my head I told myself that I was the prom queen (even though there was no prom). Once my mindset changed, I started caring far less about blending in. Instead, I focused more on connecting back to the way I'd felt about myself as a kid – when I felt confident in who I was, and what I liked.

ONCE MY MINDSET CHANGED, I CARED FAR LESS ABOUT BLENDING IN

Kids found me confusing. I'd hear them ask, 'Is that a boy or a girl?' Boys would call me a lesbian or make fun of how feminine my voice was, but they were making fun of me for things I was aspiring to, so it didn't get to me. I would hear it and think, *Okay, that means they think I look like a girl!* The only thing I really hated were the sexual jokes, because I hated being sexualised. Teens can be SO sexual, and if you're not at the same level as your peers, you can feel clueless. That was me.

I felt like the kids around me had so much more knowledge about sex, and this was a source of anxiety for me. I was so naive. At home, after school, I'd search all the sexual words people were directing my way, and I'd be disgusted by what I saw. I didn't want to be associated with those things.

I don't think older generations fully realise how numb Gen Z has become to seeing graphic content. A lot of what they might consider shocking isn't a big deal to us. We are growing up in a time where graphic content is part of our language. Gen Z speaks to each other through images; we say 'I love you' with a nude. It's how we interact and understand things.

WHEN I HIT EIGHTEEN, IT WAS GAME ON. I WAS FINALLY READY TO SAY, 'YES, I'M TRANS'

Even though I felt behind other people sexually, the fact that I finally knew where I was heading gave me so much hope. I had a game plan, and now that it was clear to me and to my family, every little thing that took me one step closer to that – whether that was wearing mascara or styling my short hair – was a comfort to me and added to my sense of who I was. Mum was as excited by all of this as I was. She'd take me shopping and help me look pretty. Dresses started coming into the mix, and I felt so empowered and READY.

When I hit eighteen, it was game on.

I was finally ready to say, 'Yes, I'm trans.'

18, GAME ON!

Top: Feeling cute 'n' happy. Bottom: Ryan's birthday dinner –
still rocking make-up from a runway show earlier that night.

YOU ARE NOT YOUR LABELS

nobody puts Baby
in a corner!

AS A KID, I WASN'T AWARE OF LABELS

playing a role in my life in any major way.

Obviously, there were the 'boy' and 'girl' labels, and I was also half-Asian, but outside of that, people were just people to me. And I assumed that when strangers looked at me, they saw me the way I saw myself: I was just AJ. But as I got a little older, I learned that labels have a lot of power, bad and good.

The school years are peak labelling years, because you're learning about how many labels exist, and also finding out which ones people are putting on you: weird, popular, chubby, pretty, sporty, gay, straight, smart, Asian, arty . . . People love putting each other in boxes, and they're afraid of boxes they don't understand. Sometimes you can even be afraid of the box you've been put in – I know I was.

boy, this doesn't feel right

I was nine when I started singing in my school's mixed choir. We put on concerts and performed at different schools, and I was living my best *Glee* life. Each year, the teachers would choose a handful of kids to sing at a more competitive level with choirs from other schools. That year, I was one of the five kids chosen.

When the day to meet my new choir came around, Mum and Dad drove me there. We pulled into the parking lot of a school I'd never seen before, and a captain of the younger years met us at the door. Everything was fine until we stepped into the music room and I saw that there were no girls in that room – only boys. I'd never been in an all-boys environment. It was so confronting.

I froze, and that was 100 per cent because, in that moment, I realised, *Okay, the world is really against me.* I was being put in a box – a BOY box! Everything shrunk. This was life telling me, *We see you as a boy, and we think this is where you belong. These boys ARE you.* The label was being shoved down my throat, and in that moment I felt like I was going to die.

My heart started racing, I couldn't think or hear, or catch my breath. I started crying and freaking out. I didn't know it at the time, but I was having a full-blown panic attack. These attacks are super scary because you experience real physical symptoms that make you feel like you're dying. Even just remembering that situation now

Top: Aged eight, when Mum took me to see the set-up for a friend's party in a fancy hotel in the city. Right: Dane and me on a visit to our biological dad. Below: Baby me!

SERVING LEWKS FROM THE GET-GO

brings some of those feelings up in me again. That's how powerful and vivid this memory is.

My parents were CONFUSED. They didn't know what the hell was going on; all they knew was that we needed to leave. I never went back to that all-boys school again, but those few minutes changed me forever, because, for the first time, I truly grasped the concept of gender. I'd never thought of it too deeply before then, but suddenly all the pieces started to fit together. Like, *Okay, all those games we grew up playing, like mums and dads, now I get it. Now I see it's how life really is.* I could feel myself being pushed towards a role I didn't want to play. But what else was there for me?

I CAN'T BE MYSELF IN A WORLD THAT PUTS ME IN A GROUP OF BOYS

In hindsight, I can see why this experience triggered a panic attack: if you live in a world that's black and white, and you feel grey, it's a scary place to live. My brain was saying, *I can't be myself in a world that puts me in a group of boys.*

From that day, anything relating to groups of boys or confrontations with boys set off a panic attack in me. And this isn't something I've fully solved, even now. What I have done is accept that we can't help the way a situation ignites a reaction in our brain. The best we can do is try to find ways of coping and calming ourselves in that moment. And, hopefully, learn to overcome these patterns of thinking as we grow and learn more about the world.

little miss shy

My behaviour and outlook on life changed so much after that panic attack. Anxiety took over the rest of my childhood and early teens, and I started feeling very critical of myself. The way I looked and the way I sounded were attracting attention, so I stopped speaking as much. Now that I knew the world only saw me as a boy, I didn't want to be seen acting like the boy everyone wanted me to be. I put my personality on mute and became less vivacious. Eventually, it got to the point where I couldn't interact with new people, or order my own food in a restaurant, and if I wanted the 'girl's' version of the McDonald's Happy Meal toy, I'd ask my mum or brother to ask the person at the counter for me – I couldn't do it myself anymore.

I stopped asking Mum to paint my nails, and do the fun themed polishes for Halloween and Christmas that I used to love. Too many people would stare. And speaking up in class? Forget it. I felt as though I was a joke to people – I wasn't someone to take seriously.

At school, my girlfriends were starting to get excited about moving on to their all-girls high school. This became another source of anxiety for me, because it was a reminder that life was pointing me in another direction. Mum reassured me that friends come and go, that this was all normal and that I'd make new friends, but deep down I knew it wasn't that simple. I wasn't upset because I was afraid of losing my girlfriends – I was upset because I wasn't going to an all-girls school. But I didn't know how to achieve that, or how to put my desires into words.

Worried by the changes she was seeing in me, Mum asked the school for help. She thought maybe my problems had something to do with learning, and my dad agreed. They were searching for ways to help me deal with these new emotions. My teachers had noticed that I'd become more withdrawn in class, so with no other obvious explanation, the adults around me agreed that I had a communication-related issue. This led to me having to spend more time in one-on-one reading sessions with teachers in the library where I'd be forced to read, and read aloud.

It wasn't like I was officially diagnosed with a learning disability or anything – the teachers were just going off their assumptions. But this type of singling out takes a toll on a child. It alters their sense of who they are, and their sense of self-worth. Reading aloud didn't solve my problems, it just put another label on me. Suddenly, I was the 'dumb' kid who needed to read to be smart. This was such a confusing time, because I knew the truth: I wasn't staying quiet in class because I didn't know how to read – I was quiet because I was afraid. I didn't want people in my class to look at me and think, *Oh, there's another boy.* I preferred being invisible.

The adults had completely misunderstood the situation, and prescribed the wrong solution. I like to think that schools are better at dealing with these types of things, now that we know more. A panic attack isn't a learning problem, and it shouldn't be treated like one.

I felt as though I was a joke to people

everything is not
what it seems

Life continued this way for a few years – me just trying to get through the days, holding on to hope that my life would get better (it did), and finding comfort from things that made me happy: Animal Crossing, my toys, life at home and the world in my head.

Transitioning to high school was all about avoiding situations that would trigger my panic attacks. Mum was right, I did make new friends, but I also stayed scared. I couldn't help linking my situation to how I'd seen people treat my mum when I was little. I thought, *People were so mean to Mum just because she looks different. Imagine what they'd do if they knew how I acted at home, what I wanted and what I truly desire from life.*

TRANSITIONING TO HIGH SCHOOL WAS ALL ABOUT AVOIDING SITUATIONS THAT WOULD TRIGGER MY PANIC ATTACKS

Health Class in Year 7 did nothing to make me feel better. In fact, it made things so much worse, because it taught me things in a single afternoon that smashed my innocent childhood expectations to pieces. In less than an hour, I was given the main bullet points about puberty, hormones, and how boys and girls develop differently. I know this might sound weird, but all of this was completely new information to me.

I'd spent my whole childhood believing that eventually things would fix themselves and I'd develop like other girls. I was so naive, and this class made it clear that there was no way to turn this ship around. Puberty was coming for me whether I liked it or not. Testosterone would become a part of my body, and I would physically turn into the man I didn't want to be. This messed me up so bad. I thought, *Holy crap! THIS is what's going to happen? Why didn't anyone tell me?* When I got home, I was so upset with my mum for not telling me. I couldn't believe this was going to happen. In that moment, I lost the connection with the future I'd seen for myself as a kid.

I resented my body for betraying me in this way, and it was around this time that I started eating to comfort myself. In a strange way, I thought the changes of puberty might be less noticeable if I was bigger – that way, I could hide my 'maleness' under a softer, more ambiguous body shape. I figured fat would solve my problems. (Obviously, that's not a healthy way to go about things, but your girl wasn't in a healthy place!)

Before long, I had a new label to add to the pile: now I was also that 'chubby' kid.

IN THAT MOMENT, I LOST THE CONNECTION WITH THE FUTURE I'D SEEN FOR MYSELF AS A KID

anxiety: my new frenemy

✺ TW! These two pages discuss self-harm. If that's a trigger for you, skip to page 76.

The year I turned sixteen is what I now call my 'blackout' year. When I think back on it now, I can barely remember a lot of it. It's this dark, fuzzy period of my life, and mentally, I was at my absolute lowest. All the negativity around the trans label was pulling me down. In the rare moments when I'd let myself imagine what it might be like if I were to accept that label, I'd find myself stuck in the belief that I had no room or opportunity to transition. I saw no way out. Eventually, I reached a point where it was all too much, and the overwhelming thought running through my head was, *I don't want to be here anymore.*

Years of struggling with my mental health were taking a toll on my personality. I wasn't feeling or acting like myself, and I took things out on the people in my life who were close to me. There were many moments when I wasn't a good friend – especially to Roxy. And around this time, I started cutting myself in secret. I'd stumbled across a few graphic posts on Tumblr that ignited a sense of confusion in me. I wondered why anyone would do that – but at the back of my mind that knowledge was brewing . . . I was asking myself, *How is that helping them? Will it help me?* Eventually, I tried it. And once I started, I kept going. I didn't do it all the time – just when I was feeling really sad or low. And it never made me

I wasn't feeling or acting like myself

feel better for long. It got to the point where I'd wake up in the morning and have a cutting 'hangover'. All of those emotions had built up and I'd feel so ashamed, and then I'd be searching online to find new ways of hiding my cuts. Most of the time, I'd wear bands around my wrist to cover up what I'd done. Nobody knew – not even my family.

IT WAS THE REALITY CHECK I NEEDED. THINGS WERE GOING TOO FAR

This cycle went on for about six months until one day at school, when my best friend at the time spotted a mark under my wristband. Later that night, she rang me – crying – asking me what I was doing. She told me she was scared for me, and that scared me, too. I felt like shit knowing I'd dragged someone else into my problems. It was the reality check I needed. Things were going too far.

Not long after that phone call, when I was feeling really low, I rang a kids' helpline instead of hurting myself. The woman who answered listened to me venting – it all came pouring out. It was the first time I'd ever told a stranger how I felt, what I was struggling with, and what I was doing to myself. Talking to her brought me back from that dark place – it made me feel present and grounded. I look back at this phase of my life like it was an out-of-body experience leading me to that phone call.

Before we got off the phone, the helpline lady asked me to call back in a few days and let her know how the rest of my week at school went. She told me I could ask for her, and I wouldn't have to speak to someone new. A few days later, I rang back to update her, and I was more at ease in that call. She told me that I could call back any time – that she or someone else would always be there to listen. And even though I never used a helpline again, I kept that at the back of my mind. Just knowing it was there if I needed it felt comforting.

Reaching out had made me feel as though I'd taken a positive step towards feeling better and healing. I wanted more of that feeling, so I worked up the courage to follow up on that woman's suggestion to see a therapist.

My mum had been seeing a therapist to talk through some problems she'd been having, and since we'd done a family session with that therapist and I'd met her, I asked to start seeing her on my own. Opening up to this therapist was an important turning point for me. Not only did she diagnose me with anxiety and panic attacks, but she also taught me how to cope with them better using cognitive behavioural therapy (CBT). The main goal of CBT is to help you to understand your thoughts so you can think more positively about things, and change your behaviour and how you react to different situations. For me, CBT did have that effect. I started identifying my triggers and learned how to reframe things, and I never self-harmed after that.

I learned how to reframe my thinking

Having official names for my problems – 'anxiety', 'panic attack' – was strangely reassuring. It finally gave me labels I could research and relate to. I spent hours reading about other people's experiences online, and I learned I wasn't alone. Anxiety is SO common, especially in the LGBTQ+ community.

the Tumblr blues

I am seriously so very grateful for this message, thank you so much, from the bottom of my heart. It is hard, but people like you give me hope :) so thank you. <3 I really do appreciate it sweetheart <3 you're so lovely xxx

Dear Charlie,

What is wrong with me? I hate feeling this way, why do I let it control me? It makes me so angry and frustrated; I can't help but feel vulnerable, I want to be free. I don't want that worry, I don't want it consuming my life and even when I think I'm fine, I find myself dying from the inside. I don't want to be a sad story;

I want to be alive.

Love always,

A friend.

hey, friend. are you out there?

In a way, finding out how many other people in the world were suffering with anxiety was comforting. I'd message people going through similar things and we'd swap stories, and that helped make me feel less alone. But it also made me realise I'm like a sponge, because I'd absorb their energy and carry it with me; it weighed my heart down, and added to my sense that the world was a shitty place. I knew people could be mean in my own little bubble, but hearing about the struggles other people were facing showed me there were mean people all over the world. It made me sad that they had to live with anxiety, that I had to live with anxiety. It was a heavy label to carry – especially at that age.

The teen years are tough enough, but going through them with the sense that you're the opposite gender to the body you're living in is next level. You're at war with yourself every single day, and so much of my anxiety was a result of this inner conflict. My therapist was helpful at a surface level, but she was treating me like every other teen, so my deeper feelings and struggles weren't changing.

One day, after my English teacher had made me aware of the trans label, I brought up trans people with my therapist. She saw where I was going with it and recommended that I see a different therapist – someone who specialised in that area. At the time, this suggestion made facing the trans label even scarier. I thought, *Shit! If she doesn't know enough about trans people to help me, then I definitely don't want to be trans. That's not who I am.* So I left it.

SO MUCH OF MY ANXIETY WAS A RESULT OF THIS INNER CONFLICT

But guess what? That trans label was kicking the door down. And. It. Would. Not. Be. Ignored. It made itself known by triggering panic attacks and anxiety. Now, I can see that my mental health struggles were a result of me not accepting the 'trans' label. But at that time, it was just too scary to accept the fact I was trans. I had no trans role models I could relate to and I was afraid of how the world would treat me. But my trans identity wasn't going anywhere, so neither was my anxiety. We were stuck together like three dysfunctional roommates.

the need for support is real

LGBTQ+ youth experience anxiety at between double and triple the rates of the general population. Tragically, suicide rates are also way higher in the LGBTQ+ community than they are in the general population. And if you zoom in on the stats for transgender and gender diverse people, they're even more shocking. A 2020 report from the National LGBTI Health Alliance in Australia shows that:

♥ 48.1 per cent of transgender and gender diverse people aged 14 to 25 have attempted suicide in their lifetime (compared with 2.4 per cent of heterosexual people aged between 12 and 17).

♥ 79.7 per cent of transgender and gender diverse people aged between 14 and 25 have self-harmed in their lifetime (compared with 14.1 per cent of heterosexuals aged 14 to 19, and 21.25 per cent of heterosexuals aged 20 to 24).

Source: lgbtiqhealth.org.au/statistics

To me, this shows how much need there is for more conversation and awareness around mental health and support for the rainbow community.

If you're struggling, YOU ARE NOT ALONE. There are places you can turn to for real help, helplines you can call, and gender therapists who specialise in counselling for the LGBTQ+ community. Some of these support services made a big difference in my life, and they are there to lean on if you need them.

Check out pages 236–7 for some supports and resources.

feel something

Feeling better and improving your mental health is all about finding things that work for your situation and personality. Here are a few go-to techniques and approaches I use. Some I learned through therapy, others are just a natural part of my life.

♥ **Know and meet your triggers:** Once you know the things that trigger certain feelings, you can build a plan of attack for how you're going to deal with them. That way, when you come across that certain person or situation, you've already thought through your response and reaction. This gives you more control and power in that difficult moment.

♥ **Don't hit pause on a panic attack:** A powerful technique that has really helped me deal with my panic attacks is to let them come. In high school, I'd bottle up my feelings and try to delay my attacks, but that's when they would end up being explosive and lead to negative things like self-harming. Now, as soon as I feel a panic attack coming on, I let it happen but I try to stay present. I start taking note of the things around me that ARE real. I talk myself through whatever I'm seeing, hearing, smelling or touching – like, *Lucy is sitting next to me.*

She's wearing a blue scarf and glasses. I can smell the hot chocolate in the mug in front of me. Remind yourself that you are present and that what's happening in your body is only temporary. It will pass.

♥ **Feel into every emotion:** I think it's so powerful to embrace every emotion, especially sadness and crying. That's how our body processes emotions – it's not healthy to keep those feelings inside. But even though it's natural to cry and express sadness, it's still not normalised (for any gender). If you're sad, I'm all about feeling it. Cry! Get it out! Don't worry about ruining the energy or bringing down the vibe because pushing that emotion down will only lead to something negative later.

If you feel sad, watch a sad movie, listen to sad songs or do whatever you need to do to connect with those feelings. I'm someone who needs to have a cry every day! Sadness, like happiness and laughter, demands to be felt.

I have a bunch of playlists on Spotify, and my most followed playlist is 'Feel something'. I've captioned it 'Sad Girl Hours'. It has hundreds more followers than my other playlists, which shows that my followers are so like me. When people DM me about their stuff I always reply, *Let's have a cry together!*

WHO said what?

I grew up in a time when being transgender, or gender incongruent, was considered a mental health disorder. The World Health Organization (WHO) classified gender incongruence as a mental health condition and saw it as a gender identity disorder. Because of that, it was listed in the same 'chapter' as mental conditions such as anxiety and schizophrenia. But in 2019, the WHO moved gender incongruence from the mental health chapter to the chapter on sexual health.

A reproductive health expert at the WHO, Dr Lale Say, explained the reason for this in a video on WHO's YouTube: 'It was taken out from mental health disorders because we had a better understanding that this was not actually a mental health condition, and leaving it there was causing stigma.'

Unfortunately, the rest of the world is slow to catch up, and that outdated way of thinking still shapes how trans people are being treated by governments and health professionals today. Gender dysphoria, which is something many trans people experience, is still classified as a disorder, but it's a separate thing. It has to do with the discomfort of being in the wrong body rather than a chemical imbalance.

Source: youtube.com/watch?v=kyCgz0z05Ik

watch this

falling far from
the apple tree

My reluctance to acknowledge who I truly was wasn't limited to being trans. I had similar feelings about being half-Asian; I just didn't recognise that for a long time. Being mixed race made it hard for people to pinpoint my ethnicity. Most of the time, I could pass for white. I hated answering questions about where I was 'really' from. And the more I saw how white culture treated and talked about Asian people, the more I shied away from playing up that side of my identity. I was afraid people would treat me the way they treated my mother, and I didn't want to be associated with the Asian stereotypes kids at school would make fun of. I hated the way all Asians were lumped together into one offensive stereotype, when in fact there are so many cultures, countries and ethnicities on that continent. There were also other reasons I felt it was easier to pass as white – and those were closer to home.

Even though I'd grown up with a Filipina mother, surrounded by her friends and culture, I'd managed to internalise racism towards my own identity, and also the Filipino attitude towards 'whiteness'. Let me explain: I love my mum to bits, but she raised us the way she was raised, and that involved pushing certain rituals and practices on us to make us appear as 'white' as possible. In the Philippines, as in many other Asian countries, there are so many creams for bleaching your skin because the beauty standard there is 'the lighter, the better'.

The Philippines was a Spanish colony for 300 years, so it has a long colonial history, and its culture is a blend of those two worlds. The language, Tagalog, even sounds more Spanish than Asian. When Mum was growing up, having a half-white/half-Filipino baby was like winning the lottery – the thinking was that those kids were more likely to be successful in life. Mum may have been full Filipina, but she pushed all of us kids to look and act as white as possible, because she wanted us to match up with the beauty standards that were part of her own culture. When I was little, I remember telling her I wanted her nose – I liked it! But she'd massage our noses to make them appear more petite and European (true story!). I've shared this story with other Asian people, and they've had similar experiences with their parents.

I HATED THE WAY ALL ASIANS WERE LUMPED INTO ONE OFFENSIVE STEREOTYPE

Going into my teens, I was confused about why Mum was pushing those white beauty standards onto us. But now I realise that she wasn't trying to be mean, it was just that she'd left the Philippines to create a better life for herself. She'd married and had her half-white babies, so in her mind, she'd done all the right things. And repeating the same little rituals with us that her mum had used on her was just another way of improving our chances in life. Even today, my mum views Western features as the most desirable, no matter how much I try to lead her away from that feeling. And she still tells me to massage my nose, but I don't. I like my nose!

It wasn't until a new girl – let's call her Blair – started at my high school that I started seeing my Asian heritage in a different light. Blair was in our year, but she was a year older than us, which made her seem cooler. She was stunning, full Filo, and the guys were obsessed with her. Everyone was talking about her.

I hadn't come across many full Filipinos, so I was immediately drawn to her. I went to talk to her and she loved my vibe, so I introduced her to my girlfriends and they all loved her. Roxy was obsessed with her and was open about her crush, but Blair wasn't fazed by it. If anything, she liked knowing Roxy had a crush on her – she was born to be the centre of attention. Being the 'popular' girl, the 'pretty' girl, the 'smartest' girl in the group – those were her labels. She was the embodiment of the ultimate 'it girl', and to be honest, her labels suited her.

I learned a lot from having Blair as my friend, but maybe the biggest thing I took from her was to take more pride in my Asian heritage. Blair was a proud Filipina, and she could tell that I wasn't as comfortable with that label. She had a way of making me feel like I was a bad Filo. Whenever she'd come over, she'd speak to my mum in fluent Tagalog, so of course Mum was obsessed with her, and Blair knew it – she thrived on it.

The way she owned her Asian identity and made it cool was a game-changer for me. I started embracing that side of myself, and seeing my differences as a positive. Her motto was, 'You've got one life, own it and make it really bold' – and that spoke to me. She taught me not to give a crap. It felt exciting to try on that attitude after spending years worrying what other people might think of me.

I started to see my heritage positively

30th June, 2013

~~~~~

No more labels for me. I am myself,
and I'm going to try not to give
a crap about what people think.
Ahaha, and I just realised I should
jot down the date before I write
something. Oops. Well,
bye for now. — A

sweater weather

LGBTQ+ labels weren't even on my radar until I was about fourteen or fifteen. Roxy was the first person in my life to question her sexuality. She was very open about her attraction to girls, and even though I admired that about her, it scared me a little because she was free and self-assured, while I was so confused and naive.

Roxy wasn't bi, but our conversations inspired me to learn about bisexuality, opening my eyes to the fact that there were more ways to express sexuality and label yourself than just 'gay' and 'straight'. Still, back then, it didn't seem like bisexuality was validated as a full sexuality in its own right, the way it is now – or at least that's the message I took away from the information I found. Instead, it was talked about like it was a stop on the way to another sexuality – a transition stage between being straight and gay, or vice versa.

Trying to understand my own feelings at that point was hard, because my relationship with my own sexuality was not an easy one. I had intense crushes on famous boys (hello, Harry Styles), and I was also attracted to boys at school, but deep down I knew this wasn't the whole story. Humming away in the back of my mind I also had an attraction to girls, but untangling those feelings from the ones I had about wanting to be a girl was tricky. I didn't fully understand my attractions, so it didn't feel right to date girls at that time – especially since I knew I didn't want to be the 'masculine' partner in a relationship. The only solution I could think of was to block those feelings. So when Roxy would talk about her feelings for girls, I'd get annoyed or try to change the subject, because it was too confronting to hear about something I hadn't worked out for myself yet.

It was only later, after my gender confirmation surgery, when I was finally feeling more like my true self, that I started to embrace those feelings and the 'bisexual' label for myself. This came later for me, and that's fine. You don't have to be quick to label yourself. Sometimes, when we rush to figure things out, we might mislabel ourselves by choosing a term that seems close enough to how we feel. But as we grow and evolve as a person, it's okay for those labels to change.

SEXUALITY IS A SPECTRUM, AND WHERE YOU FALL ON IT CAN CHANGE AS YOU GROW AND CHANGE

If someone grows up heterosexual, but then feels different attractions when they get older, that doesn't mean they weren't truly 'straight' before – or that they're 'gay' now; it just shows that we're complex creatures. Sexuality is a spectrum, and where you fall on it can change as you grow and change.

labels around the world

In some countries, Iran, for example, being gay is a crime, while being transgender is tolerated because it's considered a gender identity disorder (GID) that requires treatment. In fact, gender confirmation surgery has been performed there in huge numbers – more than any other country in the world besides Thailand. The Iranian government even covers some of the costs of the surgery for those diagnosed with GID. That may sound progressive, but it's not. Trans people still face discrimination and violence. And the reason people are encouraged and supported to transition is because it keeps up the appearances of everyone being heterosexual. Gay relationships are illegal and punishable by death.

That government would rather have a gay person go through the ordeal of transitioning (which may not otherwise have been their choice), just so they can look like they're part of a straight couple. In many countries, the LGBTQ+ labels people identify with don't just carry weight on a personal level, they're a matter of life and death. There are 13 countries where being gay is punishable by death, and about 70 where it's a crime.

Sources: glaad.org/vote/topics/global-lgbt-rights; outrightinternational.org/being-lesbian-and-trans-iran

more labels,
more peace

When you grow up on social media, it's your resource, your everything. It shows us how big the world is, and how many types of people are in it. And growing up with this wider perspective means we have more labels to identify with than our parents did, and this knowledge is power.

Older generations can try to understand this broader perspective, and they can use social media all they like, but it's never going to be the same for them, because they haven't lived their teens on it. It hasn't shaped them the way it has shaped us. Having so many labels to choose from means there are infinite ways we can describe ourselves – from the gender we identify with, down to the aesthetic we're into. They're all ways to express ourselves in the world, so it can be disheartening when a young person comes across a label – for example, 'pansexual' or 'non-binary' – that makes them feel validated, only to have an older person say, 'That's not real – it's just made up.'

I was really into Tumblr when it first became a thing, and I discovered so much new information on there, but even people at my high school would hear a label that wasn't mainstream and say, 'Oh, that's just a Tumblr thing. It's not a real thing.' But if someone finds something that speaks to them on a deep level, who are we to invalidate them? It's not right to gatekeep. It's not

Left: Mum and me at a PR event, Christmas 2017; I wore red lips all year thanks to Taylor Swift's *Red* album. Middle: Growing out my hair, aged 18. Right: Me and my friend Whitney dressing up for fun, as Cinderella and a fairy.

our place to police how other people experience the world and choose to identify themselves.

The way I experience anxiety may be different to someone else, but that doesn't mean it's not anxiety. We shouldn't need to have the exact same experiences in order to share a label. If someone feels a certain way, we should have empathy for them and acknowledge that feelings and emotions are complicated. There isn't just one way to feel something.

There's way too much gatekeeping of labels these days, even for labels that are meant to be purely for entertainment. Take Harry Potter, for example. People will actually tell you what they think your

#PROUDHUFFLEPUFF

Top: Finding a Harry Potter-themed cafe, 943 King's Cross in Hongdae, Seoul.
Bottom: Getting my Bambi hugs in at Moomba Festival, 2020.

house is. When you say, 'No, this is my house, I took the test,' they'll be like, 'No, no, no. This is you.' They take it so seriously, and all you can do is laugh because bby, it's not that deep!

There's also a lot of gatekeeping around labels in the LGBTQ+ community. And even though I've never been a true fan of labels, I do understand how finding one that fits can make you feel more validated. My labels are known, but they only have power to me. You are the only person who can allow a label to stick, and even when it does, it's always your right to peel it off and try on something else whenever you decide to. We are constantly changing as we grow, and it's not about picking and choosing for fun, it's about finding which description fits you more comfortably than the others.

The labels that were hardest for me to wear growing up were the ones put on me by other people, and the ones I refused to acknowledge, even though I knew, deep down, they were true for me. Fighting against the label that fits you is exhausting. That's why it feels so good when you eventually make peace with who you are. The right label can bring you a sense of belonging, because you finally understand where and how you fit in. As you grow, learn more about the world and get to know yourself, it becomes easier to transition away from labels you've outgrown, and towards ones that are true for you in this moment. It's never too late.

finding my people

I'VE SPENT MOST OF MY LIFE

trying to find friends who would make me feel good, accepted and seen – and in my twenties I finally found them.

Today I have amazing people in my life, and I'm grateful for them every day. There were missteps and heartbreak along the way, but that's okay. All of my experiences with people have taught me something I needed to learn about the world or myself. One of the biggest lessons I needed to learn is that you have to open up to people and accept that they may hurt you – or they may turn out to be amazing and the best thing in your life.

It's impossible to predict what role someone will play in your life, and you shouldn't go through life scouting people to play certain roles. No matter how desperate you are to be part of a *Pretty Little Liars*–style friendship group, you can't force four girls to hang out together and think it's going to be iconic. (Trust me, I tried!) Forcing relationships – friendships or romantic ones – rarely works. Real connection happens organically and often takes us by surprise. All we can do is stay open and ready for when those moments show up.

This chapter is mostly about friendships and relationships, because they shape who we are as people. But it's also about embracing the power of fictional characters and their storylines. A good amount of my childhood and early teens was spent feeling alone, confused and unsure about friendships, and while I was waiting for my people to show up, I found so much comfort and happiness – actual happiness – from characters in movies, TV shows and books. When I got a little older and went online, I found a whole other group of people I could relate to, and creators who inspired me.

REAL CONNECTION HAPPENS ORGANICALLY AND OFTEN TAKES US BY SURPRISE. ALL WE CAN DO IS STAY OPEN AND READY

I'm sure that having those characters and connections was a big reason why I was able to stay positive and hold on to the belief that things would work out for me. Somehow, I knew that one day I'd have amazing people in my life who understood me. The fictional characters I latched on to in the meantime were my life rafts – they kept me afloat until those people and situations could make their way into my life. Understanding their worlds helped me navigate mine better. I still fall in love with characters and storylines today and find comfort in them. That's the point of art – it's there to take

LOVE THESE TWO!

Top: Bambi and me at Mardi Gras 2020; it was my second year walking with Instagram's float. Bottom: Picnic in the park with Ryan.

us out of our lives and show us new perspectives. Narratives are created so we can understand ourselves and our demons better. That's why we need more diversity and representation in these forms of media. When a person or character sounds and feels more like you, it's easier to find comfort in them.

THE FICTIONAL CHARACTERS I LATCHED ON TO IN THE MEANTIME WERE MY LIFE RAFTS - THEY KEPT ME AFLOAT

It's easy to tell someone who's in a toxic situation or friendship to 'surround themselves with the right energy' or to 'go and find good people', but that can feel like a slap in the face when you're struggling. It's not always that simple. There are so many factors that can make getting away from a bad situation or person hard: age, lack of money, timing . . . A person can hear that advice and think, *How?! Tell me how I'm supposed to find that 'right' energy? And where are all these 'good' people you're talking about? I just don't see them.*

If you're reading this and you feel alone, I see you and I understand how that feels. I've felt that way, too. And I want to tell you that people are not the only answer – you don't need them to feel complete. It's true that the right people will lift you up and make life better; if you haven't met them yet, you will. Things won't always be this way, and you deserve to find moments of happiness and inspiration now.

have courage
and be kind

Some of us find strength in a quote, some of us find it in a book; I found it in a movie. Eight-year-old me was obsessed with Hilary Duff, so the minute *A Cinderella Story* came out (this was back in the days of VHS tapes), my older brother Dane rushed out to buy it for me. We watched it together, and I'm not lying when I say that movie changed my whole life. I studied that film. I must have watched it 10,000 times, and I still watch it to this day. I'll never get sick of it.

It may be cheesy in an early-2000s way, but as a child, I connected with this modern interpretation of the Cinderella fairytale on so many levels. I didn't have an evil stepmother or stepsisters telling me I was worthless – society represented that to me. I related to the way Sam (aka Cinderella) was bullied and felt trapped by her crappy situation. The way she found courage despite her situation felt so magical to me. I also admired the way she showed everyone kindness (even the villains) and managed to hold on to the belief that she was worth something, no matter how people were treating her. That gave her power, and I don't think people focus on that enough when they talk about this movie.

Some feminists discount this movie and the Cinderella story in general because she ends up with a man, and that's the thing that 'saves' her, but I guess it's down to interpretation. The way I see it, Sam has no choice over her situation and no power over her environment. Yes, she accepts her life and ends up with the prince, but the way she stays kind and stands up for herself is the thing that always stood out to me.

Watching Sam stand up for herself would make me feel strong on days I was feeling down. If a kid made fun of me for wearing nail polish, I'd come straight home to watch that movie, and instantly feel better about myself. I took the movie's messages of self-love, courage and kindness to heart. I based my whole energy and persona on what that movie taught me. I wish all kids had that something that gave them this sense of reassurance and safety, because it's so important at that vulnerable age. I'm so lucky I had it; I don't know what I would have done without it.

This movie has been a constant reminder in my life that when people do and say mean things, it's almost always down to their own insecurities and issues. I'm not saying bad behaviour should be excused – it shouldn't. But if someone is targeting you, it can help to understand that it's about them, not you. It was my jealousy that made it hard for me to show love and kindness to my little sister in the beginning, because that feeling was so strong. But I knew that I didn't want to play that role in her life, so I switched it up. And today I have a best friend for life in her. She loves and understands me like no one else.

Remember that you can decide to be the cause of someone's happiness or take it away. It's always a choice.

to kill a mocking girl

Around the time I started socially transitioning, I became obsessed with the TV show *Pretty Little Liars*. The character I most related to on that show was Hanna. Her character was the 'chubbier' one in the group of friends, and her struggle with her weight really resonated with me. When she decided to lose the weight to fit in and become more desirable and popular, I got it in my head that if I got healthier and lost weight, then I'd be more popular and more desired, too. To a degree, that turned out to be true. People definitely started showing more interest in me as a person once I started conforming to more conventional beauty standards.

THE TV CHARACTER I MOST RELATED TO
WAS HANNA ON *PRETTY LITTLE LIARS*

I modelled myself after Hanna in so many ways. I did my hair like her and dressed like her. She was the template for the style I thought I needed to have, and the types of people I thought I needed to gravitate to. The characters she dated in the show were the types of people I thought I should date. Seeing the way other characters responded to her when she became thinner and started expressing her femininity more gave me a total high, but that was soon followed by the lows of realising how stupid the world is, and how toxic this focus on looks can be.

After her transformation, Hanna's character went through an identity crisis. She had achieved her goal of becoming popular and more of an 'it girl', but who was she really? Was this new version of her even the real her, or was she just playing a character in her own life? Watching her character question these things made me do the same. And it got me thinking, *Do I want to go through life pleasing other people, or do I want to please myself?*

Like Hanna, once I was dressing and acting the part of an 'it girl', I realised I didn't want to be that person, either. It wasn't really me, and I didn't like the attention. In many ways, the show helped me work through a lot of things I was confused about during my early transition.

I know that a lot of people can relate to watching something and developing an infatuation with a character, or a feeling that they *are* that character. And that's sort of the point of books, movies and TV shows. They're designed to be a canvas you can paint yourself into, and to give you empathy for others. Protagonists are created so we can step into their shoes and live through their experiences. I was so caught up in the storylines of those four main characters and the mystery of the show that I didn't really care about what was going on in my own high school life – I was more into the lives of these fictional friends because I wanted to be them. I wanted to be part of *their* story. I don't know whether that was healthy or not, but I do know that focusing on their lives rather than my own helped get me through that time.

I found wisdom through fictional figures

my comfort characters

♥ Sam Montgomery
(*A Cinderella Story*)
——

♥ Mary Beth
Ella Gertrude
(Disney's live-
action *Cinderella*)
——

♥ Hanna Marin
(*Pretty Little Liars*)
——

♥ Alaska Young
(*Looking for Alaska*)
——

♥ Jules Vaughn
(*Euphoria*)
——

♥ Rue Bennett
(*Euphoria*)
——

♥ Wanda Maximoff
(*Marvel Cinematic
Universe*)
——

♥ Santana Lopez
(*Glee*)
——

♥ Cher Horowitz
(*Clueless*)
——

♥ Rebekah Mikaelson
(*The Originals*
and *The Vampire
Diaries*)
——

♥ Bonnie Bennet (*The
Vampire Diaries*)
——

♥ Jennifer Check
(*Jennifer's Body*)
——

♥ Charlie Kelmeckis
(*The Perks of Being
a Wallflower*)
——

♥ Hermione Granger
(*Harry Potter*)
——

♥ Rapunzel
(Disney's *Tangled*)
——

♥ Jo March
(*Little Women*)
——

my Hanna-
inspired
looks

HEY BESTIE, LET'S GET COMFY

my cosy creators

Even though I sometimes had crushes on celebrities, I found there was a wall that stopped me from relating to them. For me, finding similarities between the storylines of characters I loved and my own journey was way more exciting. But as more and more creators started coming online, I started looking there for comfort and inspiration as well. Suddenly, the people I could relate to were not only real, but also accessible. They felt closer and connected to me in some way. Even now, I learn so much from the people I follow; they give me hope, they inform, they make me laugh. Here are some of my faves . . .

My comfort/LGBTQ+ creators

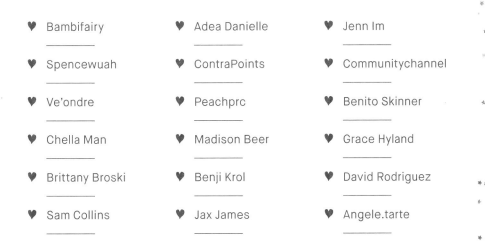

♥ Bambifairy
_____

♥ Spencewuah
_____

♥ Ve'ondre
_____

♥ Chella Man
_____

♥ Brittany Broski
_____

♥ Sam Collins
_____

♥ Adea Danielle
_____

♥ ContraPoints
_____

♥ Peachprc
_____

♥ Madison Beer
_____

♥ Benji Krol
_____

♥ Jax James
_____

♥ Jenn Im
_____

♥ Communitychannel
_____

♥ Benito Skinner
_____

♥ Grace Hyland
_____

♥ David Rodriguez
_____

♥ Angele.tarte
_____

It's important to find things that bring you happiness and spark interest and excitement for life, especially if you're going through heavy things. Obsessing over a creator or character may not be 100 per cent the right way to deal with a difficult situation, but it's better than looking for comfort in darker places, like alcohol, drugs, food, sex . . . things that can be addictive, and might end up hurting you. If something harmless helps, and you come out the other side in one piece, who cares if you watched a movie 10,000 times?

FIND THINGS THAT BRING HAPPINESS AND SPARK INTEREST AND EXCITEMENT FOR LIFE

~~always~~ will be friends

Alongside my infatuations with various characters, I also made a friend in my teen years who taught me a lot of lessons – some of which were really hard to learn. Throughout high school, my ride or die – let's call her Rachel – was my rock. We were both hanging out with the same group of girls when we figured out that we shared the exact same humour and interests. We clicked instantly and could be silly and stupid together; it was the best. Before we knew it, we were best friends doing all the things BFFs do: having sleepovers all the time, sharing everything, planning our wedding days . . .

We never, ever fought. I put her on a pedestal, just like I'd done with my friend Ava in primary school. Neither of us were what I'd call popular, but this bothered me less than it bothered her. I wish she could have seen herself the way I saw her. I'd tell her all the time how pretty she was, and that it wasn't important whether or not people at high school knew her.

Rachel was naturally creative, and she encouraged me to explore my creative side. I actually started my YouTube channel with her, and it was so much fun. The two of us (and sometimes Roxy) would film funny music videos and have a great time. Our interests stayed the same as we got older. We both loved drama so much that we decided to do a certificate in screen acting together. It was a separate course outside of school and it was a perfect fit for us.

When Rachel got the lead in our high school's musical, it was a special moment in our friendship – I was so proud of her. We were the outcasts that nobody knew, yet she'd landed this lead role and, suddenly, people at school were noticing her. And I LOVED that for her because I already thought she was one of the most talented and beautiful girls at school, and now other people were seeing that in her. I was always hyping her up.

Other students would ask her when she started at the school, because they assumed she was new, even though she'd been there from the get-go. She'd get hurt by that, but I'd tell her to take it as a compliment. I was like, 'You're talented and people are seeing you now. Enjoy it!' When the show opened, I bought tickets and went to see her perform every single night. I loved watching her shine.

After Rachel starred in that musical, we went from being the kids nobody cared about, to being better known. She became popular, and since we came as pair, I did too, by default. In a strange way, I felt like I owed her something. She had given me social currency, and that started to create a shift in our relationship.

Our friendship had always been a crazy and beautiful thing. Inside our friendship, I'd always felt completely free – but things were changing, and even Roxy could feel it. She didn't like Rachel's energy, so she started drifting away from us and spending more time with Blair. After high school, things changed even more – I'll tell you how in the next chapter.

the queen bee

When Blair started at our high school, she shook things up and got everybody talking. None of us had met someone quite like Blair before. The way she came onto the scene opened my eyes to a whole new way of existing in the world. She had major main-character energy, and I was so drawn to that. We all were. Even though she was the same grade as us, she was a year older and had her full driver's licence, which made her even cooler in our eyes. There's always that one friend who pushes boundaries and makes life exciting. For me, that was Blair. When we were together, I felt like I was living in a movie. I never knew what was going to happen. Her impulsiveness got us into tricky situations all the time, but she'd blow it off afterwards by saying, 'This is what you do when you're a teen!' She believed that the bolder you were, the less people questioned you, and in a way, this worked for her. Consequences were rarely a problem.

I'd never seen anyone use their sexuality to get what they wanted before, but Blair was the epitome of someone who knew what they wanted and how to get it. She was a stunning girl with so much confidence, and guys were completely under her spell. I liked that she also wanted me to experience life, too. She had this way of pushing me into the deep end and getting me to try things that she knew I was curious about – like dating. Even though following her lead was scary for me, I'd often go along because it was thrilling.

I wanted to catch up with her, but she was in another world – especially when it came to boys. I'd listen to her talk about dates she'd been on and think, *I need to get on that level.* She had lots of experience with boys; meanwhile, I was seventeen and hadn't been on one date yet. Since I was feeling cuter and had started socially transitioning, I decided to change that. There were no guys at school I felt comfortable asking out, so I arranged a date with someone I met online. He was in his twenties and worked at the university. When I casually dropped the fact that I was trans into our early chats, he didn't seem fazed. We arranged to meet outside the public library.

When the day of our date came around, I was excited. I took the bus into the city, but the moment it pulled up at the library and I saw him waiting outside, I changed my mind. He looked way older than me, and suddenly I didn't want to go through with the date anymore. Unfortunately, when I got off the bus, he saw me right away and came over, so I couldn't leave or pretend I hadn't seen him. I quickly made up an excuse and told him I was meeting a friend for a movie and couldn't stay long.

In total, our date probably lasted ten minutes. He kept trying to get me to stay, but I'd already sent Blair a text and asked her to come and get me. When I got in her car and told her what had happened, she said, 'You're doing it all wrong. My way is much safer.'

From that point, we'd go on dates together – only our dates wouldn't know that we knew each other. Blair and I would drive to this bowling centre that also had a theatre and a bar, and we'd each pick where we wanted to meet our date, and then we'd each go on our date – knowing where the other one was the whole time. Afterwards, we'd leave together in Blair's car. Not having to worry about the guys taking us home made us feel like we had all the power. I liked having that safety net while I was out exploring this new world of dating.

Even though we were friends for a couple of years and would FaceTime every night, Blair never got deep with me. I often felt that under all her confidence and experience, she was dealing with more than she let on. She taught me that people are complex and that you have to give them the benefit of the doubt.

That friendship was exciting, and I lived through her for a minute in time. I knew she needed me too, in some way, so it was a win–win for both of us. But I also found myself being dragged along into things I didn't want to be a part of. At some point, I sensed when it was time to get off the roller coaster.

Even though Blair may not have been good for me all the time, I'll always be thankful that I had her friendship during this time in my life. She pushed me outside my comfort zone and taught me new things. Life can send you the right people when you need them – and as long as you're learning from someone, those experiences are not wasted moments.

22nd October, 2013
'Le city stay'

~~~

This was so much fun.
Everyone had their up and
down moments but what I
truly know out of it all is
that the city is where I have
to be. The city inspires me
and one day it will be mine.
For now, I have to stick
with what I have. Hopefully
the good will come.

still don't know my name

Being thrown into the dating world by Blair opened my eyes to another side of teen life. I was feeling more feminine and ready to explore relationships a little. Up until this point, even through the anxiety and panic attacks, I'd managed to hold on to that *Cinderella Story* mentality: that I was the only one who could define my self-worth, and that how other people felt about me didn't really matter. But now, I could feel that slipping way. That way of thinking became warped by teen shows, friendship groups and the world around me – and I began to search for external validation to feel 'loved'.

Once I started getting attention from guys, I took the confidence that gave me and ran with it. I felt I needed to 'catch up'. Most of my teens had been spent hiding, and now that I was starting to express my femininity, I wanted to feel what everyone around me had been experiencing for several years already.

So I started talking to random men online. I preferred older men to boys my age, as they made me feel more feminine. And the more attention I got, the closer I felt to my femininity, and the less I felt like I was 'missing out'. Looking back, this wasn't the safest approach. And now that I know more about how the real world is, I would NEVER recommend that teens message or spend time with random strangers or adults. But at that time, I thought I was being careful enough, because my friends were across what I was doing – if I went out to meet someone, I'd tell my friends who I was with, and where I'd be. I'm lucky it worked out.

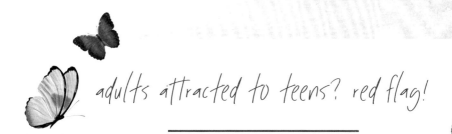

adults attracted to teens? red flag!

Now that I'm in MY twenties, I fully grasp what a huge age gap there is between the teens and the twenties. I'd never want Kiki dating someone my age, and I'd definitely question why they were trying to date a teen in the first place.

When I was growing up, the teen characters on the TV shows I loved dated older men (hi, Aria!), and it wasn't a big thing. The men weren't portrayed as creepy guys who were grooming the girls – if anything, they were romanticised. But film and TV aren't real life. It's great for teens to introduce adulty things into their lives when they feel ready – but maybe do some laundry or cook dinner, don't date grown-ass men!

Thankfully, Kiki and her friends are way more street smart than I was. They can spot the ways adults groom kids and teens. Many Gen Z-ers will see older men on apps and openly question WHY they're interacting with teens. That's amazing. No matter how mature you think you are, I promise you that dating an adult is going to be so different to dating someone closer to your age – and not in a good way.

Luckily, nothing bad happened to me, but a lot of that was probably down to my dysphoria. I wasn't ready to be sexual. If I had been, who knows how things might have gone for me.

I downloaded Tinder and went on heaps of dates just for the hell of it. I wasn't looking for a partner or someone to settle down with, and I wasn't looking to hook up, because I wasn't ready to be physical with someone yet. It was solely for fun. I saw dating as a character-building exercise – a way to find out who I matched with and what I was like in those situations. I'd try on a different personality each time to try to figure out who I wanted to be. I'd dress cute and get taken out, and in those moments, I'd feel I was getting closer to who I wanted to be when I was older. It was my way of expressing self-love.

I'D TRY ON A DIFFERENT PERSONALITY EACH TIME TO TRY TO FIGURE OUT WHO I WANTED TO BE

BUT, whenever I'd talk to guys online or on apps, I'd make it known right away that I was trans, so that it was out in the open immediately. I wouldn't make it a big moment or conversation – I'd just drop it in casually, like, 'Oh, by the way, I'm trans.' Putting that info out there before the date not only meant I was keeping myself safer, it also gave the guy time to educate himself about trans people (if he didn't already know) before meeting. I always felt like telling guys that I'm trans was a kind of filter: it showed their true colours instantly, and weeded out the guys who weren't comfortable with it. But even though I'd let them know in advance, I still spent way too many dates feeling like I was 'educating' them – talking my date's ear off about being trans because they hadn't even searched the term before meeting up (I mean, who doesn't google their date?).

be informed before you meet someone

If your date knows the basics about you beforehand, but you find yourself having to educate them about your identity in the 2020s, that says something. There's a difference between a few curious questions and ignorance. Dating reveals bad eggs, along with the good ones. Approach it with an open mind and know when to walk away, and you'll be able to appreciate the experience, even if it doesn't lead to anything.

Putting the riskiness of dating older strangers as a teen aside, I think the way I approached these dates was right for me. The way I look at it, if you want to have experiences and your intentions are clear, and you aren't using people, there's nothing wrong with going on a date for the fun of it. Every date was a learning experience because it also taught me things about myself. And for that reason, I recommend going on casual dates if you want to understand yourself a bit more. At the end of the day, we're all just out there trying to find pieces of ourselves.

If you've been talking to someone on an app and you want to meet them, remember that you don't owe them anything. Period. Doesn't matter if it's work-related, a coffee catch-up with an old friend, or an interview at a cafe. You're just two people meeting up. If you get serial-killer vibes from them, you can leave, no questions asked. Just like I did on my first date.

And if that person doesn't get in touch after, that's also okay. As much as ghosting sucks and it's rude, that's life. You had an experience, and now you can both take something from that.

dating and disclosing

Trans people, and especially trans women, learn to read the room quickly when they're out in the world. Sadly, this skill is vital for our safety, because anti-transgender hate crimes are on the rise in many countries.

If you're trans and you're meeting someone for a date, I think it's always better to tell the person that you're trans BEFORE meeting them. Don't risk doing it in person. If you do decide to tell them after you meet up, make sure you do it in a public place, when lots of other people are around – please don't wait until you're back at their apartment or you're alone with them. It's too dangerous. Your life is so much more valuable than someone's feelings about your identity.

You never know what sort of upbringing or experiences someone has had, and you can't know if they will be triggered by something you say, or if they'll act out when you disclose that information. With some men, things can turn violent when they feel that their masculinity has been threatened.

I've heard from so many girls who have put themselves in this situation, and it's truly scary. It's also terrifying when you're out in public and some random guy decides he likes the way you look and won't leave you alone. And then, when you tell him you're trans, he responds aggressively – even though you didn't ask for OR want his attention in the first place!

If you can have the buddy system or some other type of protection when you're out, do it. Always. It's sad that we need to operate this way, but this is the world we live in. The Human Rights Campaign records show that 2020 was one of the worst years on record for murders of transgender and non-conforming people, and also saw more violence against trans people in the US.

In 2020, the number of transgender people who were murdered was the highest since these figures started being tracked – though these numbers are just 'the tip of the iceberg', as so many of these hate crimes go unreported. In the US, for example, it's not mandatory for law enforcement agencies to report hate crime statistics, so many of them don't. That means the numbers we hear about aren't the full picture.

Globally, 350 trans people were killed in 2020 – and 98 per cent of them were trans women or trans-feminine people. A fifth of them were killed in their own homes. The average age of these victims was 31, and the youngest victim was just 15.

You'd think transphobic violence would be falling as trans visibility and representation increases, but it's not. It's actually on the rise. In the UK, reports of transphobic hate crimes have quadrupled over the past five years. The COVID-19 pandemic played a role in this increase, because any time there's a crisis, it always disproportionately affects marginalised groups.

stay safe!

More representation and visibility on social media is a good start, but it's not enough. I think in some ways, the increasing visibility of trans people on social media is actually stirring up that phobia and aggression. For any real change to happen, mainstream media needs to back the trans community more, brands need to back us more, and TV and movies need to include storylines celebrating trans people and show that loving them is okay. We need stories that show trans people existing beyond being a villain or a 'deceiver' towards the world. Too many trans people are killed by partners who don't want others finding out that they were in a relationship with a trans person.

And it doesn't end there. A man in Philadelphia committed suicide in 2019 after being bullied for dating a trans woman. In his suicide note, he wrote that he 'didn't want to live in a world that made fun of his love'. This is heartbreaking. It's sad that he was bullied, it's sad that his friends wouldn't accept his relationship, and it's sad that they didn't live in a place where people would accept that love and not bat an eyelid at it.

Some people say the world isn't ready, but WHEN will it be ready? People are being killed. Getting more education about trans issues into schools will help, but for now, it's on us to keep educating and do what we can to keep ourselves and each other safe.

Source: Jamie Wareham, 'Murdered, suffocated and burned alive – 350 transgender people killed in 2020', *Forbes*, 11 November 2020

November 20 is the global Transgender Day of Remembrance, which honours the thousands of transgender people who have been murdered as a result of transphobia.

what is a hate crime?

A hate crime is a criminal act – often a violent one – or other form of abuse carried out because of prejudices about someone's race, ethnicity, gender, sexuality or disability. If you are the victim of a hate crime, get to a safe location as quickly as possible. If you can, call for emergency help (see numbers below) and ask for the police. If the crime has already happened, report it to your local police and tell them you believe it was a hate crime (and why). Hate crimes deserve to be reported, not only to protect yourself (and others) from further abuse, but also to help government agencies understand the extent of the problem, so they can budget money and resources to fight it.

AUST call **000**   **NZ** call **111**   **US** call **911**   **UK** call **999**

knight in shining armour

My one-hit wonder dating streak was interrupted by a guy from the UK who I ended up seeing a few times. It felt refreshing to go out with someone who wasn't from Australia, and he was very respectful – he always asked me about who I was as a person, rather than my transition, and I loved that. He was 26 and I was 19, but I felt like a baby because I had very little experience and I didn't know what to do, or even whether we should talk about sex.

He never put any pressure on me to do anything or move faster than I was ready to, and when we did eventually kiss, *I* was the one to do it. I'd kissed guys before, but this was the first time I'd ever made the first move, and it was such an empowering feeling. He waited for me to initiate the kiss, and when you see someone looking at your lips and you know they're waiting for you, it's really sweet. Him giving me that control was such a natural, organic way to help me feel safer in that situation.

When he had to leave the city for three months for work, we put things on hold. And while he was away, I realised that I *wanted* to keep seeing him. This was a completely new feeling for me, and it made me examine my feelings more than I ever had before. There were no guarantees, and I didn't know where things would stand when he came back, but I took a break from dating other people and waited patiently for him to return. And it turned out to be good for me.

We picked things up when he got back, but he was returning to the UK and that was hanging over us. Even though I really liked him, I wasn't ready to be intimate or close with anybody until I had the body I belonged in – and that wasn't going to happen anytime soon. I told him that I wasn't comfortable doing more with him, and he was totally fine with that. We agreed it would be hard to keep seeing each other and strengthen our bond, only to have to end it when he went back to the UK, so we agreed to leave things there. I was okay with that because there was no other solution.

setting my own pace was important

After this relationship ended, I wanted to find that same energy with someone else. Being with him had taught me that going at a slow pace was healthier for me – and that dating a different person every other day and trying to fill my time with strangers wasn't helping me at all anymore.

In the early stages of my transition, I was so afraid of being alone with my thoughts that I needed that constant validation from strangers. But by filling my head with all these guys, I wasn't giving myself any room to understand that I was also attracted to girls. Letting yourself sit back, breathe, and be okay in your space – as you are – is a really healthy way of showing yourself love and kindness.

Three years later, I got a sweet message from him out of the blue – a kind of congratulations while I was in hospital recovering from my gender confirmation surgery. He was in a new relationship and a lot of time had passed, but his message meant a lot. He didn't need to send it, but the fact that he did meant I could tie a neat ribbon on our story, and close the book with a happy ending. And I knew we wouldn't have had that if I hadn't been patient with him, and vice versa.

my light in the darkness

The amazing angel that is my Bambi fairy fluttered into my life during such a weird time, and I'm forever thankful she did. Rachel and I had gone our separate ways, so I was getting more connected with people in the YouTube community, and started spending most of my time with a group of older creators. I'd just turned 20 and they were all close to 30, so whenever we hung out together, I found myself trying to act older for them and fit in with their Gen Y humour. We were at very different stages in life, but since I didn't have any real friends at this point, I was taking whatever friendships I could get.

In some ways, I felt safer with the people in that group than I had in a while. I could be expressive around them, and I liked that they lifted up my successes and were on the same path as me. But socially, it wasn't a good fit. They were social drinkers, and I wasn't a good drinker – I found it hard to control my intake, and alcohol unleashed all my insecurities. They found this amusing, and they'd laugh about my behaviour rather than worry about how I actually felt in a given situation. I blacked out drunk two times while hanging out with them, and even had to get my stomach pumped in hospital once. It felt so degrading. That wasn't the person I wanted to be.

THE AMAZING ANGEL THAT IS MY
BAMBI FAIRY FLUTTERED INTO MY LIFE

toxic group check

It's easy not to notice when something isn't right – especially when your judgement is clouded by the fun of being in a group. It's also easy to fall in with the wrong group when you haven't figured out who you are yet. That's why it never hurts to check in with yourself to make sure you're not slipping out of doing things that are true to who you are and what you want to do in life. Be real with yourself.

♥ Do the people around you make you feel safe? Seen?

♥ Do you feel little or stepped on around them?

♥ Do they value your feelings and emotions?

♥ Are they gaslighting you?

♥ Are they pulling you away from your interests or other people you love?

If a person means a lot to you, then working on that relationship is important. But if a relationship *isn't* making you feel good, then you can walk away. You aren't in high school; you don't have to see them every day. Even if you *are* in high school, it's only a matter of time before those faces become a memory rather than your everyday existence.

I will never forget when we first met!

At a NYX Cosmetics event, I went to the girls' bathroom and spotted Bambi by the sinks. She'd recently added me on Facebook, and I remembered her face, so I said, 'Oh hi, you're Bambi – you're trans, right?' She looked at me so confused. I explained that I was trans, and then started telling her about my upcoming gender confirmation surgery; I also mentioned that I was tucked inside my jumpsuit and was so uncomfortable. I'll never forget it – she said, 'Oh my god! You're tucked? I thought you had a full vag! Can I touch it?' I was surprised, but gave her a quick nod and then she patted the crotch of my jumpsuit . . . I was shocked, but also fascinated by how bold and out-there she was!

There was another trans girl, Kara, at the event. The three of us talked for the rest of the night, and even though I felt Bambi was too wild for me, I still liked being around her. I hadn't come across someone my age who was going through the same things I was – and now I'd met two other trans girls in one night! We all agreed to meet up again, and had a sleepover not long after that.

I invited both girls to come on a road trip I was going on with my Gen Y group. It was my birthday weekend and I wanted both of them there, but in the end, only Bambi could make it. I wasn't sure how it was going to be without Kara, and Bambi could sense that I was being distant about it. A few days before the trip she messaged me and asked, *Do you want me to come or not?* I replied, *Yes, you're coming!*

All I remember from that trip is that the two of us talked and laughed for the whole two-hour journey. I told the other people in the car that I didn't want to drink that weekend because I wanted to have a fun time and I was silly enough without alcohol. When we got to our Airbnb, I told the rest of the group the same thing, but the only person who was truly listening and hearing me was Bambi. Everyone else was pushing me to drink, saying they were going to kick me out of the house if I didn't get drunk; they just thought it was funny. Bambi was the only one saying, 'Guys, she doesn't want to drink!' But once I started drinking, I got drunk, and not just really drunk – depressive drunk.

The people in that group liked me when I was funny drunk, but as soon as I got emotional, they didn't want to know. I was crying because it was the first birthday I'd celebrated since my friendship with Rachel had ended, and I missed her. I poured my heart out to Bambi and she sat there thinking, *Why is this girl so broken?* She was the only one there for me that weekend, and from that point on, we bonded and became close so fast.

Even though Bambi and I had so much fun together, the start of our friendship was pretty rocky – and that was mostly my fault. I wouldn't open up to her. I just felt too vulnerable after being burned so badly by Rachel, and I pushed her away because I was scared to be hurt again. Another major issue in our friendship was that I was still ashamed of being trans. Our friendship was confronting for me because when we were together, guys would clock both of us. When I was on my own, I could pass for cis, but Bambi was at the beginning of her transition, so when I was with her, people would 'clock' her and then figure out we were both trans – and I didn't like that.

This was such a frustrating time for Bambi. She'd try to shake some sense into me and say, 'Be trans and proud! We only live this

Bambi

Top: First sleepover
with Bambi and Kara.
Above: Me with Bambi
and some of our trans
sisters, Grace and Alice.
Left: Bambi turned
me into a fairy, too!

life once!' By trying to be as cis as possible, I wasn't creating a great environment for her in that friendship. She was out there trying to live her truth, while I was trying to be a version of myself that I wasn't.

BAMBI HELPED ME COME OUT OF MY SHELL FASTER, BETTER AND BRIGHTER

Bambi brings out the best parts of me and encourages me to live my dream, while I remind her to see herself through my eyes. Our bond has been built on so many different levels, and I think that's the beauty of a true friendship. She has never made me feel that who I am is a bad thing. I was the one doing that to myself. Bambi helped me come out of my shell faster, better and brighter. I'm sure I was meant to meet her in the bathroom that day. If I hadn't been at that exact moment in my life – caught up with a group I wasn't fitting with, and feeling a little lost – I might not have given Bambi a chance. I might not have invited her on that road trip, and we wouldn't have bonded the way we did. Every little thing we do in life is connected – it's a web pulling us to where we need to be.

Bambi had the energy I wanted to be around, so the two of us wriggled our way out of that friendship group that wasn't right for us. Now, we support each other through our experiences. Our friendship developed so naturally, and is one of the best things to happen to me.

That, and meeting Ryan soon after.

prince charming

Ryan and I met by chance, in the most organic way. I was 22, and I'd had my gender confirmation surgery three months earlier. I was feeling good and was back at work at The University of Melbourne, where I was a social media manager. I was sitting outside, on a break between meetings, and Ryan happened to be on a break between classes, so we randomly started talking. When he asked if I wanted to go for a walk and get some bubble tea with him, it didn't seem strange because everyone at that uni was so friendly. I figured he probably thought I was another student.

As we walked, he randomly mentioned that I reminded him of a Victoria's Secret model, which was pretty cringey. But at the same time, I thought, *Well, that's nice to hear. At least I know he's attracted to me.* We laugh about that comment now because he's kind of an awkward guy, and it was so out of character for him to say something like that.

But this hint that he liked me prompted me to give him the full info, so I said, 'Oh, by the way, I'm trans.' I figured that would give him a chance to get out of things if he wanted to end the walk. Like I mentioned before, telling people I'm trans is a great filter, because it reveals the type of person they are. If the way they react isn't great, it tells you so much about their character – it's a nice tool to have in your belt, in a way. It's like a shitty person detector.

Ryan didn't skip a beat. He said, 'Oh, okay. Cool.' And then he moved on to the next thing and asked me what I was like as a kid.

His response was actually closer to the way girls usually respond when I tell them. (I've never had a bad reaction from girls I've been attracted to, BTW – only guys.) I really liked that about him, and when I eventually met Ryan's parents after we started dating, I understood why he'd responded that way: they're intelligent, progressive and understanding people, so of course he was, too.

Being with Ryan was a breath of fresh air, because I was so tired of being on dates where I had to inform and educate. Even though I was the first trans person Ryan had met, he treated me like a person right from the first moment. That's all I'd ever wanted.

The second time we hung out was at Sushi Train, and that was more of a proper date. I spent the whole time trying to suss him out. Ryan was different to anyone I'd dated. He wasn't my usual extroverted type, trying to impress me by taking me on some over-the-top amazing date. Usually, I'd find myself infatuated after those dates, and talking about those guys non-stop. But Ryan was introverted and didn't make too much of an effort at all at the beginning. At first, I wasn't sure what that meant, but it became clear that he cared more about our conversations than he did about showing off or trying to be something he wasn't. And I liked that.

I found myself thinking, *He's a sweet boy, but I don't know that I see a whole future with him.* I knew I liked spending time with him, and at the back of my mind I was also thinking about my new choochie. I finally had the body I'd dreamed of – so taking it for a test drive was definitely on the agenda. I'd never considered virginity a big thing; I always used to say that if I'd been cis, I would have lost my virginity in high school because I'm such a curious person.

Top: Ryan and me at the state library in 2020 – going strong after two years.
Bottom: With Ryan at a Lauv concert.

My dysphoria was the only reason I still had my V-card. I'd hated my body so much that I couldn't do anything about my virginity until it matched how I felt inside. And now it did.

I was realistic, though; I knew that sex for the first time was going to be awkward, no matter what. It wasn't going to be some wonderful epic scene from a movie. And I thought, *Okay, if Ryan is my first time and it doesn't go anywhere after that, I'll know that I did it with a nice, cool dude. He's sweet and respectful, and I'll be happy with that decision because I'll be connected to his energy for the rest of my life.*

For our third date, he cooked me a full meal, and I thought it was the sweetest thing. No guy had ever done that for me before. Ryan turned out to be the perfect guy for me. He's so in touch with his feminine side, and that's so rare. He isn't fazed by things other guys are fazed by, and he doesn't waste energy trying to be overly masculine – he's just himself and it's so easy. As we spent more time together and our relationship developed, this was a major learning for me: relationships don't have to be hard.

My mum and my stepdad always had a tough relationship. They argue, but they also love each other a lot. And I thought that's how love was for a long time. It was only after meeting Bambi and Ryan that I realised it doesn't have to be that way. You don't have to base your own relationships on the ones you see growing up. Being in a relationship or friendship should feel like being in a team – like you're nurturing each other. You want to feel good when you talk to that person. You shouldn't have to hide parts of you to make them feel better.

People show love in different ways, so knowing what you value and communicating that is important. If you value time and your partner spoils you with gifts, you're not going to get what you need in that relationship. How can your partner know what you value if you don't tell them? In a book called *The Five Love Languages*, writer Gary Chapman breaks down the five different ways he believes we show and receive love. Each of us relates to one of these languages.

1 Words of affirmation
_____

2 Quality time
_____

3 Receiving gifts
_____

4 Acts of service
_____

5 Physical touch
_____

In the first few months of our relationship, Ryan and I discussed our own love languages. Being open about what we each needed from that early point was so good for us. It's rocky roads for Gen Z when it comes to relationships, because we live in a culture that is all about hook-ups and temporary things. But it's okay to admit you want that one person to pour your heart out to. It's up to you to define how you want to be in a relationship – and even if it ends, you'll still walk away having learned something. You can't predict whether someone is endgame, side character or temporary love. But you can be sure that they'll shape who you are going to be in the future in some way.

I'm all in!

> **NEVER LET THE FEAR OF STRIKING OUT KEEP YOU FROM PLAYING THE GAME**
>
> *Babe Ruth*

I FIRST HEARD THIS quote in

A Cinderella Story, and it instantly became one of my all-time favourites.

Turns out the movie's writers actually borrowed the quote from an old baseball player – but it will always be connected to Cinderella in my mind. I stuck it up all around my childhood bedroom, and if you'd flicked through my journals or scrolled through my Tumblr in my teens, you would have seen it there, too. I lived by this quote. It guided the way I approached all of those challenges – those curveballs – that life threw my way.

In baseball, a curveball is a pitch that goes in a totally different direction than the batter expects it to, and is hard to hit. In life, a curveball is a moment or event you don't see coming; something that turns life upside down. Either way, those curveballs up your chances of striking out, or failing. But curveballs and strikeouts are a part of life – they're unavoidable. Some can be hard to live through, but I've learned that you CAN live through them. It's not the curveball that defines you, it's how you react to it that matters.

IN LIFE, A CURVEBALL IS A MOMENT OR EVENT YOU DON'T SEE COMING; SOMETHING THAT TURNS LIFE UPSIDE DOWN

That's why I've always loved that quote. It reminds me that I can't avoid challenges. Even if I'm scared, I still have to play the game. Ignoring or turning your back on curveballs is dangerous. They could hit you, or even follow you around for years, and that might end up being worse than facing them head on.

There's power in facing things head on, and there's power in missing and then saying, 'Okay, I missed that one, but I'm going to hit the next one.' Staying in the game has taught me that setbacks usually come with some sort of reward or happiness at the end – but you've got to stay in the game to find it.

my sweetest downfall

Without a doubt, the biggest curveball I've ever had to deal with came in the womb – being born trans. As a kid, I knew there was something different about me. Every night I'd go to sleep praying I would wake up in a girl's body and be able to live the rest of my life like that. For years, I'd say the same kind of prayer – but slowly, I started asking for less. I started saying, *If making me a girl is too hard, please just give me long hair*. Or *Please give me a girl's wardrobe*. Or *Please don't let people be mean to me when I start dressing like a girl*.

I was negotiating with whatever higher power was out there. I didn't know if I was praying to the god my mum was teaching me about or some other being, but I felt like somebody was listening. And slowly, in my teen years, it dawned on me that life *was* kind of giving me the things I'd prayed for. It was just giving them to me gently. It was a shock to realise that my childhood prayers were being answered.

As each step in my transition presented itself, I felt myself moving closer to the person I was inside. Many people don't realise how many hurdles there are to overcome before your physical self can match up with your identity. Within that one giant curveball of being trans, there are a thousand other curveballs to face. They come one after the other – until, eventually, you're on the other side. And then, they keep on coming!

The long process of medically transitioning – which many trans people decide *not* to do, for many reasons – begins with hormone therapy. Some trans people take hormones and choose to stop their medical transition there, content with looking and feeling more like the gender they identify with. Some have 'top' surgery, where they either get breast implants or have a mastectomy to remove their breasts. Others have facial procedures to help them achieve more feminine or masculine features. I had a procedure known as a tracheal shave to reduce the appearance of my Adam's apple. (Many cis people get tracheal shaves as well.) And finally, some trans people, like me, have gender confirmation surgery to change their genitals to match the sex they identify with.

To qualify for gender confirmation surgery, you have to stay on hormones for at least a year and live your life as the gender you want to transition to. For me, just knowing those male hormones were being blocked from taking over my body was a huge thing. Having female hormones flow through my body for the first time was a game-changer – I started feeling more in sync with myself, and looking even more feminine than I already did.

For me, one of the most difficult aspects of the whole surgery process was having to stop taking those female hormones one month before the surgery – because depriving my body of those female hormones meant I was literally going through menopause. Imagine experiencing those feelings in your early twenties! It's like, *What the heck is happening, this doesn't make any sense!*

body and mind finally in sync

Testosterone blockers are really harsh in any trans girl's body, but I found them particularly bad, and I experienced a lot of side effects. In a way, this was just another confirmation that I really needed the surgery. I would have had too many problems if I'd had to stay on those testosterone blockers for the long term.

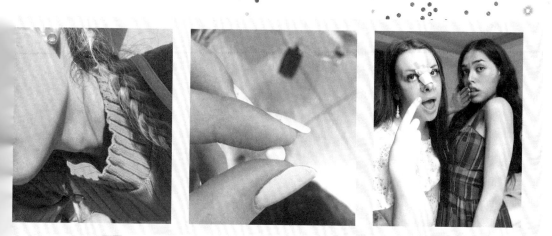

Left: The 'before' picture I had to send the doctor in Thailand doing my tracheal shave surgery. The technique I wanted (where the incision is made under the chin rather than on the throat) was only performed in Thailand and the US.
Middle: My first oestrogen pill – inspiration for the 'T-Girl' colour in my makeup palette.
Right: With Bambi, post-nose surgery, in Seoul, Korea, 2019.

it's about aligning, not 'reassigning'

Gender confirmation surgery has been known by lots of different names: gender-affirming surgery, sex change operation, genital reconstruction surgery, sex realignment surgery, sex reconstruction surgery and bottom surgery. Until recently, it was also referred to as gender reassignment surgery, but now the words 'confirmation' or 'affirmation' are used instead of 'reassignment', because medical professionals know that it's about confirming and aligning with the gender you already are, rather than changing it.

transitioning: what is the process?

Talk about curveballs! Here are some of the many, many steps involved in transitioning. Every trans person's transition will look different – there's no one way to do it.

social transitioning

Social transitioning involves presenting in public in your identified gender, either occasionally or all of the time. To do this, someone may take some (or all) of the following steps:

♥ Changing your clothes or hairstyle

♥ Packing – trans men may use padding or a prosthetic penis to achieve a more masculine genital shape

♥ Tucking – trans women may place their testes into their inguinal canal, and then wear tight underwear (or something called a gaff) to hold them in place and give them a feminine genital shape

♥ Binding – trans men may wear a super-tight chest garment to flatten their breasts

♥ Wearing breast, hip or buttock prostheses – trans women may wear these under their clothes, or in their bra, for a more feminine shape

- ♥ Coming out to parents and family members, partner(s), friends, classmates, co-workers
- ♥ Changing your legal documents to reflect your chosen name, gender identity, and the pronoun you use

medical transitioning

Like social transitioning, medical transitioning is also a very individual process, and for some trans people the steps may include:

- ♥ Hormone therapy – a young trans person may choose to take hormone blockers to stop puberty in its tracks while they go through the steps needed to transition
- ♥ Gender affirming surgeries, in areas such as the chest, face and/or genitals
- ♥ Hair removal (from the face and/or body)
- ♥ Speech therapy
- ♥ Sperm or egg storage, to preserve a trans person's fertility

Never, ever self-medicate – especially when it comes to hormones. See your doctor before you take anything.

Source: transcare.ucsf.edu/transition-roadmap

don't forget to live while you're waiting

If you're going ahead with gender confirmation surgery, my biggest piece of advice would be to not put your whole life on hold in the year leading up to it. Don't get me wrong, having to mentally prepare for something like this is a HUGE thing – especially when you feel you should have been born that way in the first place. But letting it consume you isn't the answer.

When I look back, I feel I wasted so much of that year before my surgery being caught up in my transition. Nothing else mattered. I became more isolated and got down on myself. And when you're not really living your life, you risk getting depressed. That's what happened to me, and it was scary, because I hadn't felt that way since high school. That's why I always try to keep that favourite quote in mind and that mentality about staying in the game, no matter what. If I allow myself to go into that dark space, it can take me right back to that time when I was still hiding and sad.

Do whatever you can to stay present in life outside of your transition – and keep up with whatever's going on in the lives of the people who matter to you. It might be hard, but you've got to take just as much care of your emotional life and mental health as your physical body, or they'll deteriorate. Having a major surgery really puts this into perspective.

30th January, 2013

~~~

Nothing seems like it is getting better. Every day feels like a walk through a desert. it's tiring and after a while, it starts to hurt. But you have no choice but to keep moving! I know this ain't no desert, this is real life. No matter how much you walk, are you really getting anywhere? So why don't we just wait? NO! Because waiting will do nothing.

designer choochie

After a few months of hormone therapy, which I started when
I was eighteen, I was feeling happier and more beautiful in my skin
than I ever had. I'd wake up feeling so good, but then I'd go to the
bathroom and be forced to confront the genitalia I'd been born with.
It was a punch to the guts every time, and a constant reminder that
I still wasn't who I needed to be to feel at peace in my body.

Before I could be approved for gender confirmation surgery,
I had to prove that I was in a sound state of mind and that I met
the psychological criteria for this procedure. The doctors also had
to feel sure that I'd have enough support around me before and
after the operation, to ensure that I'd be able to heal properly
and do all the after-care that would be necessary. As part of this
process, I was required to attend multiple therapy sessions with
a psychologist and a psychiatrist to convince both of them that
I was a female, and that my gender dysphoria was so bad that
surgery was my only option.

Each trans person's dysphoria will be different. One trans
person may feel fine with the genitalia they were born with, and they
may not want surgery. That wasn't me. My dysphoria was extreme.
It weighed on me so heavily that I felt like I couldn't live my life in
that body anymore. Pulling my life apart for these people who didn't
know me felt scary, but so much was riding on their approval, and
I was terrified that they were going to say no.

Thankfully, they said yes.

Once I was approved, I locked in a date for the operation a year later. That's a long time to wait, but a lot of things needed to fall into place before it could go ahead. And of course, there was also the money factor to work out, because no matter where you live in the world – this surgery isn't cheap.

In Australia, our government's Medicare system pays for around $4000 of the total cost. That's helpful, but when the full cost of the surgery can be as much as $30,000, it doesn't cover much. There's no public hospital option for this surgery, only private – and you can't have the surgery unless you have top-level private health cover.

Dealing with the insurance wasn't easy. In Australia, there's no line item or box for gender confirmation surgery that you can tick on a form. It's not covered by insurance. Instead, certain parts of the surgery fall under the same categories as other procedures that *are* covered, such as removing something malignant, like a cancerous tumour, from the genital area. This is basically a loophole that surgeons use to help trans patients get more of their surgery costs covered. But try explaining that to an insurance rep.

Having to talk about the intimate details of my surgery to people at my insurance company was so difficult and invasive. I couldn't believe that's what I had to do – it was such a private thing to me. But I wasn't going to get my surgery unless my insurer approved it.

If any one of the people I dealt with – my health insurer, those two doctors, my surgeon, the Medicare people – had said no at any point in the process, I wouldn't have been able to have my surgery, at least not in Australia. Every one of these people dictated whether I was going to be able to live my life. It was heavy to not feel in

my day HAd come!

Top left: 2018, right after surgery. Right: A quick OOTD selfie before they put me under.
Bottom left: Sitting up in bed the day before going home.

control of my fate. The complicated approval process and red tape around the insurance makes an already difficult situation so much harder than it needs to be.

Even so, I feel lucky to have gone through this process in Australia. I know that it's so much harder, more expensive – or even impossible – in other countries. I also know that I got lucky with the surgery experience in general, because my surgeon, Dr Andy Ives, was so good at managing the pain that I literally felt little to nothing during or after. On a scale of one to ten, my pain was a four at its worst. Most of my recovery was spent sleeping, passing out or spaced out on the pain meds they were giving me. The only pain I felt was when he was checking on something, or the nurses were changing my dressings or taking out the catheter. And as hard and invasive as it felt to have nurses down there, just knowing that part of me looked the way it was supposed to gave me such relief, I didn't even care – my dysphoria was finally quiet, and that felt amazing.

WE CAN'T HOLD ONE TRANS PERSON'S SURGERY EXPERIENCE TO BE THE DEFINITIVE EXPERIENCE

The nausea when coming off the anaesthestic was also pretty bad, but again, it was manageable. I've since met five other girls who've had this surgery with the same surgeon, and their experiences were very similar to mine. But I've also heard from trans girls in other countries and cities who've told me their surgery is the worst thing they've ever experienced.

To me, this is a reminder that we can't hold one trans person's experience to be the definitive experience. A trans friend of mine recently had her surgery done in Canada, and the Canadian government paid for the whole surgery. She messaged me after her surgery saying, *This is so painful! You told me it wouldn't be painful.*

I felt so bad for her, and I replied, *Baby, you did it in a different country with a different surgeon.* So many factors determine how things play out. Surgeons have different techniques. Bodies respond to drugs differently. Surgery in a private healthcare system might differ from surgery in a public system, and the after-care may be managed differently in terms of how the pain meds are distributed. It's impossible to predict what someone's surgery or recovery will be like, or how easy it will be for them to take care of themselves afterwards. For example, after this surgery, every patient is given a pack of medical-grade dilators in different sizes and told to dilate several times each day during their recovery, starting with the smallest size. This is to ensure the patient doesn't lose depth or width in their new vagina. It's a super-important step, and making time to follow these instructions as often as you're supposed to takes discipline and commitment. It's all a journey.

surgery is different for every patient

Having this surgery brought peace to my brain and daily life, but it hasn't meant that my dysphoria has completely vanished. It's still a cloud hovering over me, making me feel grey at random moments, and reminding me that I won't ever truly be complete, even with the choochie I have.

But in saying this, every single body is different, so who are we comparing ourselves to? Yeah, I'll need to dilate for 30 minutes, three times a week and take hormones for the rest of my life – and yes, it took me two months to be fully able to move around and have my body back – but we all have to do certain things to take care of our bodies; that's what makes us human.

There are positives and negatives to everything. My body will never be perfect, but it is mine and I'm happy with it.

RIP to my youth

Beyond a shadow of a doubt, one of the fastest and hardest curveballs that comes as you transition from your childhood into the teen years is social media. One day you're a kid living your life. Things are simple and your friends are your friends. Then you create your first social media profile, and everything is different. The language you use shifts, and the way you communicate with other people changes. You go from catching up with friends in person, and getting to know them gradually, to having video calls, messaging and communicating with pics 24/7.

Using a laptop or a phone, you can absorb someone's whole life story in a matter of days, and share intimate thoughts and stories with people you've never met. Bonds get formed quickly, and feelings can be intense – and that's confusing when you don't have that much life experience to draw on. This was a major curveball for me. I found it hard to understand the depth and the power of the feelings I'd have for someone based solely on online interactions. It was so hard to know how to separate those feelings from real life.

As a teen, I felt lots of things for people online. Connections could seem deep, but then, when we'd finally meet up in person, all of those feelings would be out the door, and I didn't understand how that could happen. Nobody explains that to you – how you can build relationships through images and words online, yet feel no spark or connection in real life. It can really mess you up.

Anonymous asked:

dear bestfriend

Dear Best-friend,

I cannot express the love I have for you, you
are my everything and the other half to me.
You are amazing in my eyes and I admire you
so much. You are going to do great things, you
really are; I just know it. I can't wait for us to
leave high school :'D you are wonderful and
beautiful in every way possible, please believe
that :) I love you so much >3 xx

Love always AJ

Anonymous asked:

dear person i like

Dear person I like,

I love you so much that it hurts. I should just
move on because I know it could never happen,
but there is something about you that I love.
I don't get what it is, all I know is that I really
like you.

Love always AJ

Thanks to Tumblr, I
ended up having a new
crush every few weeks
– solely because I'd
stalk someone's page to
the point that I thought
I knew them personally.

Now that I've been online for longer, I don't place such intense expectations on the people I interact with there. I share positivity and give love to people who interact with me, but I don't expect anything deep in return. That said, I do feel like the people who follow me are part of me, because I know we're similar in some way. Whether they're in the community or not, they follow me because an aspect of my personality resonates with them. But how we are online – in DMs and posts – is usually a heightened version of who we are in real life, and we can easily hide certain things about ourselves. For example, when people meet me in real life, they are often surprised by how anxious and awkward I can be in person. They get to see that I'm not confident 24/7. Online, you can feel close to someone, while also knowing there's more to them that they aren't showing you.

girls.

In the months leading up to my surgery, I started questioning my sexuality. I'd always got along better with girls, and I found myself wondering if I was supposed to be with a female energy. I was torn, though, because at that point, lesbian couples in the media always seemed to be portrayed a certain way: there was always one woman in the couple who was a little more 'masculine', and the last thing I wanted was to be the masculine energy in any relationship. Because of this, I felt that I needed to be with a man to feel feminine.

Around this time, I became friends with another YouTube creator, Tonia, and she was on the same page as me. Neither of us knew how to label ourselves, and we weren't calling ourselves bisexual, but we would always talk about it.

One night, we ended up at a club and I spotted a gorgeous guy. I started trying to get his attention, but he wasn't vibing with me. I'd catch his eye, but then he'd disconnect the line. Eventually, I noticed that he was standing next to the most stunning girl.

Later, as the two of them were holding hands and on their way out of the club, she touched my arm as she walked by and said, 'You're stunning!'

'Girl, no YOU! Congrats, you got him. He's the hottest guy in the club.'

She gestured for me to come closer, like she was going to tell me something, and then said, 'You're really pretty. He's okay, but I don't want to leave with him.'

'What do you mean? Then don't leave with him!'

And THAT was when she pulled me in and kissed me.

not all curveballs are bad!

The guy was standing behind her and was so confused. I was also confused – but happy! Just like that, she changed her mind and decided she was staying with me. He left on his own, and the two of us spent some time talking to each other. We were vibing so well and were so comfortable with each other. This encounter opened my eyes to the battle I'd been having with my femininity. It took being in that moment to realise that being with another feminine energy didn't have to mean feeling any less feminine.

boys.

A month before my surgery (and several months before I met Ryan),
I was invited to VidCon Australia. VidCon is this big event that
started in the US where digital creators and fans come together
for a few days of panels, workshops and events. And as a YouTuber
with a growing presence, I was invited to speak on some panels that
year. I was beyond excited, because I'd been planning to go anyway.
Now I was going as a panelist!

Over the course of that weekend, I developed a crush on
a Canadian bartender at the creator events. I really liked him –
everyone could tell – and I looked forward to running into him. The
two of us had so much in common, and the conversation just flowed
every time we talked. He was sympathetic about the anxiety I was
feeling about speaking on panels. One night, riding high on the
energy of the weekend, I thought, *I'm feeling good, I'm going to
invite this guy back to the hotel to hang out with me and my friends*.
Even though we'd had a few great conversations, I hadn't told him
I was trans, but I wasn't worried. It wasn't a date, just a bunch of
friends hanging out.

Back in the room, the two of us were deep in convo when
I realised that Bambi was explaining, to another girl just a few
feet away from us, the type of hormones we take during our
transition. I looked at him, not knowing what to say, but knowing
that he'd definitely heard and that his mind was probably going
crazy. Later, when I asked him if finding out I was trans had

shocked him, he said, 'Oh, it's okay. I did a Google search on you, so I already knew.' (Phew!)

He told me that even though he didn't know much about the LGBTQ+ community, he still wanted to see me and go on a date, so we did. I let him know that I was off my hormones because I was having surgery in a month. And he understood and was supportive throughout the whole thing.

For the rest of that month, he'd come over and we'd have sleepovers. In the days after my surgery, he checked in on me a bunch of times and wanted to come and see me, but I wouldn't let him. I felt too gross – I had unwashed hair and had been lying in a bed for days. That's not the look I wanted at the start of a relationship!

Once I was recovering at home, he started coming around again. My family loved him, and he'd spend time with my younger brother, Sean, and play video games with him. With everything going so well, I'd locked it in my head that once I healed, this guy would be my first time. We'd even talk about the fact that the three-months post-surgery point was technically when I'd be 'fully recovered'. (In theory, you can start introducing exercise and start using your new vagina for sex as early as six weeks after surgery, but my surgeon had recommended that I wait a little longer for my body to tell me when it was ready.) We talked about trying out my new vagina for the first time, and he was curious. I was too. It felt like we were on a good path.

And then, out of nowhere, he ended the whole situation. He told me he didn't understand his emotions, and that he needed to come to terms with things. And with going back to Canada hanging over him, he didn't want to pursue anything that would make it deeper. I understood all of that – but to me, it was so strange. I didn't understand why someone would entertain and nurture a connection the way he had, only to end it all so abruptly. If he hadn't felt like he was able to end things before the surgery, why had he continued to see me through my recovery?

I was angry. I wished so badly that he'd just cut off our relationship before my surgery so I could start life fresh with my new vagina and have new experiences with new people. Instead, I finally had my vagina, but now I felt shitty. Yet another guy had changed his mind – only this time it was worse because I wasn't a confused and scared teen anymore. I felt better and more at peace with myself than I ever had, and more deserving of love than I ever had. One minute this guy was hanging out with my family, ready to be my first time and make it special for me. The next, he bounced. I hadn't seen it coming.

When I first received his text message, I had a good cry about it and let my feelings out. But once that was done, I switched things up and said to myself, *You've just gone through major surgery and come out of your cocoon. You are finally a true version of yourself, and life officially starts from this point.* I wasn't about to let this guy bring that energy down. So I changed my mindset and moved on.

you accept the love
you think you deserve

Of all the guys who have hurt me, and of all the times I've cried over a breakup, none of them have ever come close to the pain I felt at losing Rachel. That's one of those curveballs that nobody prepares you for. Friendships are built on different foundations than romantic relationships. Nobody goes into a friendship thinking the other person might hurt them or leave, so if that love and trust is betrayed, you're blindsided. You literally lose a part of who you are in that breakup.

Once high school ended, things between us got complicated. I was finally able to start medically transitioning, and I don't think Rachel understood how difficult the process was going to be for me. A lot of my eighteenth year was spent going to medical appointments and doing things related to my transition. As the hormones did their thing and I began feeling more comfortable in my skin, I found that I was less willing to play the supporting role, or the 'plus one'. I was ready for more.

Another thing that was shifting had to do with money. I'd been going to interview after interview, but still had no job, which meant I had no money. Meanwhile, Rachel had found a good job and was earning plenty of money. When it came to hanging out together, she wanted to go out, but I couldn't afford to. Instead, I'd invite her round for sleepovers or offer to cook her dinner, and I think she took that

actual broken heart

the wrong way, that I was trying to keep the focus on me – but really, I was broke and starting a difficult medical process. I just needed her to be there for me.

Rachel had made a new friend at work who was also in the LGBTQ+ community, but I didn't like him very much. He had a catty personality, and I noticed that his energy was rubbing off on her. Whenever she'd start bitching about people, I'd call her out on it and tell her it wasn't cool, and that the things she was saying were literally bullying. She didn't like me calling her out that way, and even though we kept hanging out, I started feeling that something was 'off' between us. On the surface, things seemed normal – we were still doing lots of things together and talking all the time – but under the surface, we weren't right, and I knew it.

IF THAT LOVE AND TRUST IS BETRAYED, YOU'RE BLINDSIDED

One night, when we were having a sleepover, I noticed her phone lighting up like crazy. She was fast asleep, and when I reached over to get her phone, I saw it was her friend from work. I thought, *Okay, let's see what this person is saying* – I honestly thought maybe they were in danger. So I unlocked her phone and read the messages. (Yeah, I know that isn't right, but I knew her password and I never imagined I'd see what I saw.)

Let me tell you, the texts I read were a SHOCK to my life, to my body, to my heart. I will never be able to explain that feeling, other

YOU'LL GET OVER A CRUSH, BUT A FRIENDSHIP BREAKUP WILL HAUNT YOU

than to say something inside me broke in that moment. The pain was so intense. I wouldn't wish it on anyone. His texts were about me. Horrible, mean words about me, about the food I was cooking for her, how annoying I was, how she should leave my house. But what hurt the most was that she wasn't defending me or doing anything to stop him. In fact, she was egging him on. The time stamps on her messages showed that she'd been hanging out with me while a lot of these texts were going back and forth. I was beyond confused. I just kept asking myself, *Why would she keep spending time with me if this is how she feels?* I knew that our friendship had felt different for the past few months, but the two of us never fought. I still thought we had all this love and admiration for each other.

There I was, standing next to my best friend – my only friend, really – and losing her completely. I'd been so focused on my transition that I'd drifted away from everyone else except her. My brain was shouting, *What movie is this? I don't want to be in this film anymore!* I went and slept in my sister's room and cried so much. The next morning, Rachel left the house and then called me later. She said, 'What's up? You were really upset when I left.'

Quietly, I came clean: 'Your phone was going off for ages while you were sleeping, so I unlocked it and read the messages.'

'How dare you!' she shouted. She was so angry, and told me it was an invasion of privacy, which it was – but even as she was getting mad at me, I could hear in her voice that it was dawning on her what I'd read. She broke down and told me she didn't know why she'd said those things. She said sorry and all the other things people say when they think they're going to lose you, and want you to forgive them, but I couldn't process it. Things were different now.

Rachel tried to fix our friendship. She'd show up at my place with cakes, and when I finally got a job, she'd send flowers to my work. You'd think I would have written her off completely, but I didn't. She was my only friend. I didn't feel that I could drop the friendship completely. In a way, I compare it to an abusive relationship – people

things can change in an instant

Opposite page, from left: During a lunch break at my office job, aged 21; with Roxy at my princess party; on a road trip with Ryan, finding Paddington Bear at a market. Below, from left: Waiting for Bambi to get out of nose surgery, in a hospital in South Korea, 2019; Mum and me at a PR event – she loves an excuse to dress up; Bambi and me at my brother's wedding, 2021.

might tell you to leave that person, but it's not that easy. You still love them. You're invested in each other, and in a screwed-up kind of way, you think you deserve that treatment. I did. I thought that this was the best friendship I was going to get, so I hung on for longer.

Neither of us were finding our new dynamic easy. My YouTube videos had grown a following, and I was getting invited to a lot of events in the city because of that. Even though outwardly, Rachel was trying to be supportive, she was showing signs of not being happy for me. When I invited her to be my 'plus one' at a Sony listening party for Zayn's new album, she ended up getting really drunk. The event was supposed to be all about the music. Everyone was being chill and wearing headphones to listen to the album, but she was in the bathroom crying, and drawing attention to herself.

I REALISED I'D HIT SUCH A LOW POINT. I THOUGHT, WHAT AM I DOING? THIS ISN'T A FRIENDSHIP

When we got back to the apartment we were staying at, she threw up in the room. I took care of her, put her to bed, and as I was kneeling on the floor cleaning up her vomit, I realised I had hit such a low point. I thought, *What am I doing? This isn't a friendship*.

From then on, I decided to drift away from her. But I still couldn't seem to let her go completely. When I was invited to be a panelist at VidCon, I gave her one of my free tickets so she could experience it, too, and come and support me. But when that weekend came, she was nowhere to be seen. I called. I messaged. She ghosted me. Late that Sunday, she called to explain that she felt it was too overwhelming, that it hadn't made sense for her to go.

This was the last straw for me. I was done having to tone down things I was excited about so she wouldn't feel a certain way. There'd been a point where I would have done anything to keep her as a person in my life, but that time had passed. Rachel was telling me what I already knew: she was incapable of showing up for me the way I'd been doing for her since day one. It was really sad.

I pulled back from her completely after that, and eventually, she stopped getting in touch as much. Occasionally, she'd reach out and apologise again, and I always listened to what she had to say. But I knew that she was still hanging out with that friend from work who'd been so mean, and that never sat right with me.

where's the empathy?

As I've reflected on the whole mess of that night with the texts, I've realised that it also hurt because that bullying had come from a guy who was out and proud in the LGBTQ community, and that stung extra. I wanted to shake him and say, *Where's the empathy? Don't you realise that the way you're treated as a gay man – it's ten times worse for a trans woman? Why can't you show up and be there for your community a bit better, instead of tearing us down?*

You'll get over a boy. You'll get over a girl. You'll get over a crush. But a friendship breakup will haunt you. It's like a death without a dead body. Making peace with the fact that you won't be friends with that person because you don't fit together anymore is painful.

That loss is a big part of who I am – but so are the things I've learned from it. Now, I know what I'm worth, and I don't accept less.

ACCEPTING

WHAT

IS

there's only one you!

ACCEPTANCE OF YOURSELF,

a situation, another person, feels so good – but it isn't always easy to reach.

When you're growing up and forming your sense of self, every casual comment adds up. A racist comment, a transphobic joke, a slur whispered under someone's breath . . . it all piles up in the back of your brain, feeding the negative perceptions you hold about aspects of your identity. That's why coming out to yourself is by far the hardest thing to do. At least it was for me. Those negative messages I'd absorbed about trans people created a disconnect in me: I was trans, but I would tell myself that I wasn't trans, because I couldn't accept that label. For so long, I refused to accept the truth.

My transphobia came mostly from the media, but it also came from the things I'd hear my peers and people at school say in passing. And not just about trans people. There were lots of general slurs towards the LGBTQ+ community. My brain took these in and said, *If I'm trans, then that means I'm included in that community – and why would I want to be a part of a minority group that's hated?*

But when I was finally able to overcome my internal struggles and admit that truth to myself, I felt like a million boulders had been lifted off me. I could breathe! The world suddenly felt less against me. Things became so much easier and started falling into place. Lying about who you are, or playing a role that isn't you, can only ever drag you down. And the further you sink, the harder it is to swim back to the surface.

LYING ABOUT WHO YOU ARE, OR PLAYING A ROLE THAT ISN'T YOU, CAN ONLY EVER DRAG YOU DOWN

There's safety and protection in hiding who you are, but there's no freedom. That only comes when you are able to let go of your fears and allow yourself to be vulnerable. YOU get to decide how you truly feel, and what you want for yourself above everything else. There's power in that, because people who aren't being true to themselves are vulnerable. They don't understand their own wants and needs, and that makes it easier for people to bully, control and manipulate them.

Once you accept who you are, it's easier to stand up for yourself. Your mind can't be changed as easily, and you're less likely to let other people dictate how you should live your life.

acceptance starts at home

One of the things I feel most grateful for in my childhood is the acceptance and love that I was shown by my parents and family. I know that it's a huge reason why I was able to hold on to positivity and hope throughout the lowest points in my journey. During that time, I needed someone to show me that this was just who I was in that moment – it didn't mean this was going to be me in five years' time. Luckily, my therapist and my family were there for me.

But the sad reality is that so many people don't have anyone to pull them back from the edge. The lack of information for trans people and their families makes it harder for them to find support and be accepted. It's getting better now, but there was a definite lack of info when I was young, and the high suicide rate among trans people we talked about on pages 78–9 reflects that.

Even if someone does get through their tough times and their transition, society is a hostile place for trans people. This can be true within families, too. And when there's a lack of acceptance in a family, that shows up in tragic ways: suicide stats are higher for trans people who have parents who don't accept them. I look back at my transition now, and think, *Yes, I went to dark places, but if I hadn't had my mum as my rock to support me and not judge me, I don't know how things would have turned out.*

Family support is such an important part of the acceptance puzzle. As kids, we respect and take in our parents' opinions above everything else; we're shaped by their views at a young age, and we internalise the lessons they teach us. The fact that I grew up believing in my mum's version of God meant that later, when other people told me God would see me as an abomination, I didn't take that on. I saw God through my mum's eyes, and I believed that she was right and those people were wrong.

I hate that so many people don't get this same acceptance from their parents. I hate that they have to try to find the love they weren't given outside of their family. This puts them on a difficult path to find people and things to fill that void.

If people in your life aren't accepting of you, please know that you don't have to subject yourself to their judgement forever. There are other places you can turn to for real help, and other supports you can lean on (see pages 236–7). And if you can't move on from those people right now in this moment, know that you will be able to, one day soon.

Maybe those people will come around, maybe they won't. If they don't, they're not worth it. You don't have to excuse someone's behaviour or stick around just because someone is blood related. If they want to work towards the issues they have, they can. You don't have to let them hurt you in the meantime.

Sometimes, knowing what NOT to accept is the best life skill to develop.

mahal kita (I love you)

Aunty Zeny has had my back since day one

Although I never had a coming-out moment with my family, I do remember, as a teen, telling a close family friend, Aunty Zeny, who lives in the Philippines, that I wanted to transition. I felt a sense of safety with her. She understood me and had always accepted me – even when I didn't know who 'me' was.

I began forming a bond with Aunty Zeny when she visited her daughters in Australia and Mum introduced me to her. Aunty Zeny would come into my room and tell me how much she loved my facial features. She was always telling everybody that I'd be a model one day. She saw light in me when all I felt was darkness. She would often refer to me as *maganda* (Tagalog for 'beautiful'), and that would make me feel so special because no one referred to me as 'beautiful' besides my mum.

As I grew older, Aunty Zeny would remind me that I was capable of big things and to never let my heart change. I spent a few days with her in the Philippines one year, and as we headed for the mall in a taxi, she had a nap. I looked over at her, and the way she looked so peaceful warmed my heart. She's a pure soul who gave me the courage to open up about how I truly felt on the inside.

AUNTY ZENY WOULD REMIND ME THAT I WAS CAPABLE OF BIG THINGS, AND TO NEVER LET MY HEART CHANGE

Later, during this same trip, I told her I was going to start my medical transition when I returned to Australia. She was so excited for me, and asked if I wanted to go to her favourite hairdressers the next day – she said it would make me feel *maganda*. I said yes, and from that point, she was one of the main supporters of my transition. She was also the first person I told when I knew I was going to have gender confirmation surgery, and she wanted to help me as much as she could. Aunty Zeny has truly helped me feel seen and accepted every time she has walked gracefully into my life, and I'm always so thankful to have met her.

starring role

One of the best things about accepting yourself and rising above the fear of letting the real you out is that you have more empathy for other people. It's like your vision becomes clearer. Suddenly, it's easier to see how someone else's life might be a full struggle, too. I experienced a full-circle moment like this not long ago, with someone who'd given me a hard time in my teens.

I'd met this person – a gay man – when we were both teens taking a two-year acting course. That course was the first time I'd spent time with teens outside my school – kids who were theatrical, creative, and had different outlooks and backgrounds. It was so much fun, and I felt safer being myself than I did with the kids at my school. And because it was an after-school class, I was even able to wear my Hanna Marin outfits.

I thrived in this environment and loved the lack of judgement I felt there. So when we were assigned to read for a character described as 'gender-neutral', I decided I was going to play this character as a woman. I got a new dress and wore this beat-up blonde Lady Gaga wig that I thought looked kind of real. I'd been losing weight, and starting to feel more feminine, so I felt really cute.

Rocking up to class that day felt scary because I wasn't sure how people would respond to me dressed as a woman. But the fear was in my head. Nobody batted an eyelid! The girls loved my dress, and the guys didn't question it at all. They said stuff like, 'You look really good', and 'You pull off this look.'

I loved being part of such an open-minded group

I GOT A NEW DRESS AND WORE THIS BEAT-UP BLONDE LADY GAGA WIG

The teacher came over and said, 'Oh, you look great. Are you making the character a drag queen?'

'No,' I said. 'Does this look like drag?'

'No . . . it doesn't. Oh! Is the character trans?'

I'd never heard an adult actually say the word 'trans' out loud before, and I didn't know how to respond. It had only been a week or two since Roxy had asked me if I was trans, and I was still fighting that label. But my teacher loved this take and said, 'That's cool. That will add a lot of depth to this character. Everyone, take notes and ask AJ if you have questions.' I spent the rest of that class feeling the best and most confident I'd ever felt in any class.

But one student wasn't having any of it. This guy wasn't out or anything, but the rest of us assumed and accepted that he was gay. He had a very feminine energy and was incredibly flamboyant and extra – we loved that about him. Nobody judged him. But whenever someone would insinuate that he was gay, he'd get really defensive and insist he was straight.

On this day, he was the only person who wouldn't accept me. He followed me around class, picking on me, and just wouldn't let it go. I asked him to leave me alone, but instead he moved himself next to me so he could aggressively question me: 'Are you wearing make-up? Who wears make-up? You can't do that, you're a boy, that's disgusting.' And 'Is that an actual dress?'

Finally, one of other guys in the class (a white, cis guy) said to him, 'Dude! AJ looks hot. Just leave it. Why do you care so much? It's not hurting you.' That shut him down instantly, and he never bothered me again.

LIFE ISN'T ABOUT HIDING - IT'S ABOUT BEING YOURSELF AND BEING AROUND PEOPLE WHO CELEBRATE YOUR LIGHT

Later that year, he dropped out of class completely. I had grown to hate being around his judgey, negative energy, so I felt relieved to see him go.

A few years later, when I was further along in my transition, I went to a club with Bambi and locked eyes with him. I looked different, but I could tell he recognised me, because he was trying to avoid making eye contact. He looked exactly the same, only much more fully himself. He was out with a group of gay friends, and he seemed lighter . . . freer.

unexpected ally

That cis guy in my class didn't have to say anything in that situation, but I appreciated that he did, and I've never forgotten it. He saw something happening and decided not to be a bystander. The fact that he was secure in himself and not bothered by me dressing as a girl showed strength, and the fact that he was secure enough to speak up and defend me showed even more strength. Moments like this can make such a big difference in someone's life – so never underestimate the impact you could have. Having this other student accept me and be an ally in that moment changed my perception of cis guys. Until this moment, I'd felt threatened by all straight guys – like they were out to get me or make fun of me. This exchange taught me that I could be friends with cis guys, and that they weren't all out to hurt me.

When we'd been in class together, I caught glimpses of that same carefree personality trying to break out, but he'd always pull it back. Watching him in the club that night, it was obvious that he'd accepted himself.

It's beautiful when people show you who they really are. Life isn't about hiding – it's about being yourself and being around people who celebrate your light.

Seeing him out and proud melted the bitterness I had towards him. Instead, I was able to imagine why he'd behaved that way towards me. I went over to him and said, 'Hi, you look happy, and I just want to say that I'm happy for you.' I think we both found closure in that moment. It was never as simple as him being mean for the sake of it; he'd probably been fighting against who he was, and seeing me express more of myself – and be supported by the class – had been too confronting for him. Who knows what type of home he came from, what experiences he'd had, or how much internalised homophobia he'd had to overcome to get to a place where he could be at peace with himself.

The twin struggles of coming to terms with your sexuality and your gender identity are huge. These two struggles are separate, but they're also intertwined, and you can't come to terms with who you are and start loving yourself until you untangle them. This process can be messy, and it can uncover negative perceptions hidden inside you that you weren't even aware of – beliefs planted in your mind by society, religion, your family . . . the list goes on. It's a delicate web, and all of those things impact how you feel about yourself. I had so much empathy for him because I'd done that work, too.

wasian

PROUD TO BE FiLO!

One of the most surprising byproducts of coming to terms with my identity was embracing the fact that I was half-white, half-Asian. Being trans had been my main identity struggle since I could remember, but coming to terms with my shame about being trans also made me confront my embarrassment about being biracial.

Sometimes, it's only when you put one demon to rest that you're able to accept something else about yourself. It's a web – you examine one thread, and slowly find you're pulling the threads of the other parts of your identity, until eventually it all unravels. It wasn't until I was an adult that I acknowledged that I'd been hiding my mixed-race heritage because I was afraid of being seen as Asian. And this fear had shown up in some strange ways.

As a kid, I'd watched the 2000s version of *Charlie's Angels* many times because I loved how those three female characters were the opposite of damsels in distress. The only issue I had with the movie was Lucy Liu. I couldn't understand why an Asian-American woman was in the movie with two white women. I hated her character.

SOMETIMES, IT'S ONLY WHEN YOU PUT ONE DEMON TO REST THAT YOU'RE ABLE TO ACCEPT SOMETHING ELSE ABOUT YOURSELF

Later, as a teen, I started learning about the importance of representation, and I read articles about how important Lucy Liu's casting in that movie had been for Asian culture. She was one of very few Asian faces in mainstream Western media at that time, and she helped move things forward. But as a kid, I hadn't felt represented by her, I'd felt exposed. My feelings were clouded by what other kids (white kids) would think of her. Even if I had liked her character, I would never have admitted it – I would have been too afraid other kids would think I must be Asian if I liked Lucy's character.

I also didn't think that having Asian features was desirable or pretty, so I put the two other women above her. Even Drew Barrymore's character, who was more of a tomboy, was more appealing to me than Lucy's feminine character. Uncovering this

Five murals were created across Australia for the theme of Mardi Gras 2021, 'Rise'. I was one of three creators featured on the Melbourne mural by Rory Lynch-Wells. Such a surreal moment seeing this type of visibility.

how do you actively deprogram yourself?

Once you recognise the negative messages and viewpoints you've internalised, it's important to establish why you feel that way. Where have those perceptions come from? Once you know the answers, you can start to address and correct them. Without doing this work, it's going to be hard to fully accept yourself and others, because those internalised phobias are just going to keep popping up. It takes a while to shake them off, especially if you learned them at a young age. But it can be done, and it is life changing. Here are a few things that I found helpful.

♥ Don't allow people who don't understand what they're saying to shape your thoughts or cloud your perception of yourself.

♥ Search for more positive voices and listen to those.

♥ Know that how the media portrays a type of person or group of people isn't 'truth'. It's just a reflection of how the person writing the script or telling that story sees them. You don't have to take that viewpoint in. You don't have to accept it.

racism in myself was pretty shocking, and trying to pull it apart and figure out where it had come from was very confusing.

I came to see that my fear of being seen as Asian came from the same place as my fear of being seen as trans: I was afraid of what other people would think. Even though I grew up with an amazing, beautiful Filipina mum and spent most of my childhood surrounded by her Asian friends, food and culture, negative perceptions about Asian people and society's underlying preference for 'whiteness' STILL outweighed the positive things that I was experiencing all around me. How messed up is that?

TODAY, I COULDN'T BE MORE PROUD OR THANKFUL FOR MY ASIAN HERITAGE. DIFFERENT IS BETTER!

It wasn't until I met Blair in high school that those feelings started to shift for me. Blair was the first person my age to show me that it was possible to be Asian, proud of it, AND also be the things society tells us we should strive to be: powerful, beautiful, desired, charismatic. The way Blair celebrated her culture and even used it to her advantage was incredible to me. Today, I couldn't be more proud or thankful for my Asian heritage. I know that *different is better*.

new leaf

As soon as I started medically transitioning, I was able to comprehend that I would eventually feel better in my body. My brain and body weren't fighting anymore, and my physical self was starting to align with how I truly felt.

I don't know if people realise the powerful role that hormones play in determining who we are, but it's huge. Once I started controlling this aspect of my body, I was able to turn the testosterone way down, and enjoy a life fuelled by oestrogen.

Within a couple of months, I found that I was able to evaluate situations more clearly because I was starting to *feel* the way I was supposed to, all along – like a woman. I no longer had a woman's mind controlled by male hormones, and I wasn't getting caught up in those stereotypical testosterone traits of aggressiveness or being on edge. I noticed that I wasn't as impulsive, and I had far fewer sexual thoughts, which was a huge relief, because I'd always hated not having control of those.

bye, bye boy hormones

Now that male hormones are no longer dominant in my body, those ways of being feel foreign to me. In a way, I'm grateful for the window I had into that world. I've experienced what it feels like to be in a body dominated by male hormones, and because of that, I can see how hormones drive how guys think and behave. Just FYI, this isn't me excusing boys behaving badly – we all have a choice about how we behave – I'm just saying I understand better than I might have otherwise.

Top left: Christmas cupcakes with Kiki. Right: My 'hair extensions' era – I was obsessed. Bottom left: The first time I had my hair bleached professionally.

Women are generally more emotionally intelligent, and I used that to my advantage in my transition. I found I was able to tune in with myself better and be more aware of how I felt. I was able to feel more comfortable in my emotions and thoughts, because I knew that whatever I was feeling was aligned with how I was always supposed to feel.

setbacks on the way to self-acceptance

At nineteen, I was four months into medically transitioning and on the road to accepting myself, but that road was still a rocky one. I'd been working in retail for a while, and I needed money to fund my surgery, so when a job came up at an upmarket store with an older clientele, I went for it, even though it wasn't exactly the type of store I was used to.

I'd been growing my hair out for a long time, but it was still pretty short. Even though I didn't think I was able to pass as a cisgender female yet, I wasn't being misgendered by strangers – I was passing as female. I'd also made the switch to using the name Avery-Jae, so when I went for this job interview, that was the name on all my application forms.

When being trans didn't come up during the interview, I didn't think to mention it. But after I got the job, I explained to my new manager that some of the paperwork would have to wait because I was in the process of legally changing my name, and that I was waiting for my new birth certificate to arrive. She had assumed I was just another girl fresh out of high school, and she didn't know how to handle the fact that I was trans.

Her opening suggestion was that we just fill out all the official forms using my dead name (the name I'd been born with) – but I said absolutely no way. So instead, she asked me to simply introduce myself and never talk about being trans or bring it up while I was at work. She explained that there were a lot of older women working there, and they wouldn't understand. Her request seemed reasonable at the time. (FYI, it wasn't. It also wasn't legal.) When she said, 'People don't need to know', I thought she was right. She was the older adult, and besides, I *wanted* to pass as cisgender. Yet again, I was going off what I thought *other* people wanted.

I started a few days later, and kept the fact that I was trans a secret at work. I did that for a couple of years, which is such a LONG time! And for a lot of those years, I was riding the major hormonal roller coaster of hormone therapy. Essentially, I was going through a second puberty, not to mention the stresses of the pre-op approval process, all while pretending to be the average girl next door.

When another young girl got hired, we became close and I told her my secret. She accepted me without question. Being at work felt like being on the edge of a cliff, where I could be found out and pushed off the edge at any moment. I didn't want to be outed at work, because I felt that it would cause a scene and upset my co-workers, and that my manager would find a way to make it all my fault. Plus, I liked the older women I worked with, and I didn't want them to feel awkward – or, worse, hate me.

I was sure my cover was blown one afternoon, when a man came in with his two young sons. As I was helping him, I noticed his youngest son staring at me in the way that toddlers stare at people – dead on, not breaking eye contact. I was convinced this kid knew that I was trans and that he was going to expose me in front of everyone in the store.

I tried smiling at the toddler, like, *See! I'm a nice person. Please don't ask your dad if I'm a boy.* But he was fixated on me. As they were leaving the shop, he asked his dad in the loudest voice, 'Daddy, why does that lady look Chinese?'

I swear I almost fell to the floor with relief. The dad was embarrassed and made his son apologise, but I was so grateful that he hadn't clocked me that I couldn't care less. After they left, my manager came over to check on me and I told her everything was fine. I hadn't been offended by it. Kids that young just say what they see. They're not that deep.

BEING AT WORK FELT LIKE BEING ON THE EDGE OF A CLIFF, WHERE I COULD BE FOUND OUT AND PUSHED OFF THE EDGE

I *was* clocked once (at least I *think* I was) in the worst way. Late one night, an older man came into the store. It seemed as if he knew that I was trans. He started saying things like, 'I like girls like you', and it was so scary. He gave off predator vibes, but I had no idea what to do. In retail you're trained not to be rude to customers, so it can be hard to draw the line when you start feeling unsafe.

I tried directing his attention back to the items he was looking at, saying, 'I don't know what you mean. Would you like these or not?' But he wouldn't stop with the creepiness. As I put the items away, he grabbed my wrist and told me to meet him in the parking lot after my shift. I pulled my arm back and ran to the staff room.

know your rights

Discrimination comes in many shapes and sizes, and when you consider the fact that, in Australia at least, transgender people have an unemployment rate more than twice the national average, you have to assume that discrimination is playing into that on some level. Knowing what your rights are – especially at work – is so important.

When it comes to LGBTQ+ rights, employment law is changing and evolving constantly to catch up. It's always a good idea to educate yourself about your rights, wherever you live. Bottom line: everyone should feel free to be who they are and feel safe at work.

March 31 is the International Trans Day of Visibility, which celebrates the contributions of transgender people and raises awareness of the discrimination faced by transgender people worldwide.

The store got busy, and by the time my friend was able to come and check on me, I was distraught and in tears. We called security, who thankfully stood outside for the rest of the shift. The next day, when we told my manager what had happened, she turned it on me. She asked what I'd done to let this man know I was trans, and said something to the effect of, 'Whatever you were wearing yesterday, don't wear it again. And whatever you were doing on that shift, don't do it again.' She tried playing this off as her way of protecting me, but telling someone to hide who they are and then blaming them for things they have no control over is not protection.

this ain't it!

My friend thought the way my manager was treating me was so fucked up. But in a weird way, I felt like I owed her. I excused a lot of her behaviour because she'd given me a job when I needed one.

Even though working at a place where everyone saw me as a cis woman was empowering in a way – after all, I'd spent my whole life wanting to be seen that way – I could feel part of my identity slowly slipping away. I wasn't able to fully be myself or even talk about my life the way the other women at work could. All of my important life experiences were thrown out the door.

Hiding in this way really set me back when it came to accepting myself, because the acceptance I had in that workplace was based on lies. It's one thing to say, 'We're all the same' or that 'We can all live in this world equally', but that's not real life. Our differences make us who we are and shape our life experiences, and it's GOOD to embrace that. We shouldn't have to hide or neglect who we are to make other people feel comfortable. Hiding who I was made it impossible for me to fully accept myself.

being stealth is only good if it's YOUR choice

For many reasons, a trans person might choose to be stealth at a job and not disclose that they're trans – and that's okay. It's a private matter. What's NOT okay is when someone in a position of power tells someone that they have to hide who they are, or that they cannot disclose a part of their identity. By doing this, that person is saying they don't accept you, and that others in that workplace won't accept you, either. This is bullying, and besides being unlawful in Australia, it's also not a healthy – or safe – environment for anyone to be in.

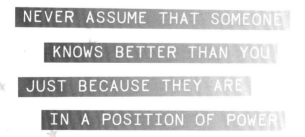

NEVER ASSUME THAT SOMEONE KNOWS BETTER THAN YOU JUST BECAUSE THEY ARE IN A POSITION OF POWER

FREE OF MY SHELL!

Top: Bambi and me making TikToks responding to JK Rowling's tweets.
Bottom: Walking with the Instagram float at the 2020 Sydney Mardi Gras.

out and proud

The next time I applied for a job, I applied as my full self – no secrets. It was for a social media position at The University of Melbourne, and I used my online platforms as my portfolio. Everything I was, and everything I'd been through over the course of my transition, was right there on YouTube for my potential employers to scroll through.

When they shortlisted me for the job, not only did they know that I was trans before the interview, they actually LIKED that about me! They had a work culture that celebrated inclusivity, and they knew that I'd be able to bring a new perspective and unique experience to their team. I was encouraged to voice my opinions and share my stories, and the people I worked with wanted to listen.

this was a big plus for me

This was such a change for me. I never thought that people at any job I would ever have would want to know or be interested in my story. But this environment attracted people who were more socially aware. And when they found out they were going to be working with a trans woman, they did some research before meeting me and educated themselves about trans people. Because of that, I was able to settle in quickly and feel comfortable that I was surrounded by people who understood a little about who I was.

When I took time off to have my gender confirmation surgery, everyone in that office was so respectful and asked the right questions. This just shows that environment means everything. Work shapes the way that you perceive the world. It's sort of like school in that you're spending all day there with the same people, so how you feel in that environment affects how you feel about yourself. And sometimes, it's only once you're in a place that embraces difference and accepts diversity that you realise how much easier it is to feel comfortable in your own skin.

acceptance can come from the most unexpected places

My friend from the retail store had a dad who – according to her – was really against the LGBTQ+ community. She told me that when he saw gay people in public, he'd be scared of them because he was so homophobic. She still invited me to their house all the time, though. And I'd sleep over there.

After I'd been to their house a few times, she told her dad that I was trans . . . and that changed his whole mind! He saw that I was a good friend to his daughter, and that was enough to change his perception of the trans community. He accepted me completely – he'd just needed to meet someone who could challenge his perception and show him there was nothing to be afraid of. That was a sweet surprise, and it wasn't the only one.

While finishing off one of my last shifts at the store before moving on to my university job, I decided that I wanted to leave

love to see growth like this

the women there with no secrets. So I opened up about the fact that I was trans, and I told them that I was getting my gender confirmation surgery the following year. And guess what? Not one of those ladies was angry, disgusted or horrified, like I'd been told they would be. It was exactly the opposite. They were kind, and curious, and so excited for me.

NOT ONE OF THOSE LADIES WAS ANGRY, DISGUSTED OR HORRIFIED, LIKE I'D BEEN TOLD THEY WOULD BE

They were also very confused about why I'd waited so long to tell them, and surprised when they found out the reason. One of the older ladies was especially empathetic, and said, 'That must have been so difficult to keep inside the whole time when you were starting your transition.' She couldn't believe I hadn't opened up about it.

For nearly three years, my manager had told me that these ladies were 'too old to understand' and that they wouldn't be accepting of me, but that was simply not true. This just goes to show that someone's opinion of how other people will feel says more about who *they* are and what *they* feel. You can't make those decisions for other people. Everyone needs to be given a chance to prove who they really are.

toxic valentine

Before my surgery, I dated a really sweet guy. He was a bit older than me, and we had a good relationship – he wasn't fazed by the fact that I was trans. We only butted heads when it came to his view of relationships. He was very traditional in that way – ready to find a good job and 'provide'. He'd talk about how he didn't want me doing much in the way of work in the future. But I had goals of my own, and I'd think, *Yeah . . . I don't know about that.* It was a big turn-off for me, but still, he was nice, and I wasn't thinking too far into the future.

But since I knew he *was* thinking long term, I was upfront about the traditional things I couldn't give him – mainly kids. But again, he was totally fine with that. After all, many cis women can't have kids, either. Eventually, he wanted me to meet his parents, and I was up for it. Even though he was excited about it, I could tell he was putting a lot of pressure on this meeting. I told him I'd do my best to fit in with his parents, but he was still on edge. And a week or two later, he casually told me I couldn't tell his parents I was trans. 'Sorry,' I said, 'say that one more time.' I was shocked, and thought, *What does he think I'm going to do? Run up to them and say, 'Hi, I'm AJ. I'm trans!'? And why is he ashamed of that?*

He told me his parents had never met a trans person, and that they were very religious. I explained that I also had family who were religious, and that sometimes it takes meeting a person and seeing how they interact with life to make people realise, *Oh, they're not the abomination I've been taught to believe they are.*

That didn't change his mind. I asked what he'd do if his parents found out the truth (all they'd have to do is google me!), but he had no game plan. I told him that the consequences of them finding out later would be way worse, but he didn't see it that way. If anything, he positioned me meeting his parents as a big moment in *his* life. For him, it was his way of telling them he was considering marrying me. This didn't sit well with me, either. It was as if he was saying, 'Put your trans identity aside and I'll promise you marriage one day.' I thought, *Sorry! Life don't work that way.*

Obviously, I said no to meeting his parents. Although he tried to mend things between us, the tone of our relationship had totally changed. If he couldn't be proud of where I'd come from or who I was as a person, it was never going to work for me.

When someone who 'loves' a trans person asks them to keep their identity a secret, it puts them at risk that people might react badly or violently when the truth comes out. Or, worse, it puts them in danger if that relationship ends and that ex-partner doesn't want people finding out they were with a trans person. I'm not saying this would have been the case with my situation, but it shows how easily one introduction can snowball into more lies.

If I'd been younger, I (sadly) might have agreed with the idea that I should just transition and live stealth. Many trans people do just that. But by this point I knew that wasn't how I wanted to live. People might say, 'Why do you need to call yourself trans when you could just call yourself a woman or a girl?' But being a trans woman is not the same experience as being a cis woman – it's an experience that stands alone. A partner who loves you should celebrate that.

there are always more things to accept

When people DM me now and ask, *How do you accept yourself?* or *How are you so confident?,* I tell them that I don't have any simple answers. I write back and say, *I know you don't feel things make sense now, but whatever you're feeling now, it will change. You will close this chapter of your book. Pain does eventually leave and end, and you won't feel the same next year. You'll go through different eras of yourself. You'll upgrade.*

It's okay to reflect and admit you weren't the best version of yourself at a certain point in time. That's normal! Once you accept the good and the bad about yourself, you'll see that you have the power to put whatever you want into your life.

Now that I'm in my twenties, I'm trying to make peace with my teen years. I'm trying to accept and be okay with the fact that they weren't full of the teen experiences I wanted to have. I didn't have

IT'S OKAY TO ADMIT YOU WEREN'T THE BEST VERSION OF YOURSELF AT A CERTAIN POINT IN TIME

a high school sweetheart, and I didn't go to school dances because I didn't want to be there unless I was wearing a pretty dress. On one level, I regret not going to those things when I had the chance, but I also know that not going was my way of protecting my soul.

I'm learning to accept that the vision that I had for my teen years was not meant for me. Instead, I feel like I'm living that high-school sweetheart relationship now, with Ryan. I also have that friendship group that makes me feel validated, and I get to dress up, feel beautiful and do fun things. Only now, I'm fully me.

Opposite page, from left: With my sister-in-law, KC, at her wedding to my brother; with Ryan after his wisdom teeth were taken out; Moomba Festival 2020 with Kiki. Below, from left: Ryan and me at my brother's wedding; selfie with Ryan and my half-sister, Kali; Bambi and me looking fancy at a PR event in 2019.

DARE

TO

DREAM

in the spotlight

WHEN I LOOK AT MY LIFE TODAY,

it's hard for me to wrap my brain around how I'm living.

If I could travel back in time and show my younger self who I am now, their jaw would drop, because the things that are happening for me today are so far beyond what I ever dreamed possible. When you're in a body that other people find amusing, and you're the 'chubby' kid people make fun of, you never feel you'll be taken seriously.

Not only was I not at home in my own body, but I also felt so far from the beauty standards I saw around me. I was never the 'crush', or the first person to be chosen – I was a stop along the way and never the destination. There was always a prettier girl or a more desired person in my friendship group. And to be honest, I made my peace with that and I was okay with being someone's third or fourth option.

But as I started losing weight, growing my hair longer and dressing more feminine, I noticed people started responding to me differently. I was eating healthier and putting a little more effort into how I was presenting myself in the world. Nothing major – just paying attention to the make-up I was using and what I was wearing. It wasn't like I was spending lots of money – I didn't have any money to spend. But I'd go thrifting and choose cute looks to fit my evolving style.

I didn't realise how much those little lifestyle tweaks would change things for me over time, but taking better care of myself gave me a respect for my body and myself, and that helped my confidence, so I came out of my shell more. The further I got through my medical transition, the more this confidence grew, and the more the compliments and attention kept coming. It was like I pushed through to a different universe.

switching the lenz

When I started feeling pretty and a little more confident, I became intrigued by the idea of doing a photo shoot. Mostly, I wanted to know how it would feel to be photographed. I'd heard of arrangements called 'time for print', or TFP, which is where aspiring models offer their time in exchange for a few professional photographs. The model gets a few free pics for their portfolio, and the photographer gets a model for their project at no cost – it's a win–win.

Over 18s only!

When I turned 20, I decided to go for it. I found a Facebook group for local photographers and models and posted a few selfies on there, saying, *Hi, I'm not a model, but does anyone want to do a*

FiNd THAT Good LiGHT

Left: My first time wearing a bikini, after gender confirmation surgery.
Top right: Just after dying my hair brunette in 2019.
Bottom right: My Lady Gaga wig phase – I loved that wig!

shoot or whatever? I'm really chill. I was SO nervous posting that. A few photographers reached out, and one of them had a nice vibe, so I agreed to do a shoot with her. These TFP shoots are only for adults, so if you're under 18, you should be bringing an adult with you, and the photographer should ASK you to bring one. If they don't, red flag! My first experience with this type of arrangement was really positive, though. It gave me a taste for being the person at the centre of the action, rather than the one on the sidelines.

Because I'd studied photography and media in high school, I was used to being behind the camera – that felt comfortable to me. But when she started taking the photos, I was surprised how free I felt. I felt connected to the camera, but in a different way.

WHEN SHE STARTED TAKING THE PHOTOS I WAS SURPRISED HOW FREE I FELT

This time, I wasn't the one pushing the buttons and making the decisions, and there was a vulnerability in that. I was also feeling vulnerable because I was way more dysphoric than I am now. But I had a sense that anything was possible, so I decided to work on being more comfortable in my skin and push myself out of my comfort zone more often. I just knew I wanted more of that feeling.

By the time the shoot was over, I was buzzing. When the photographer showed me the pictures, I thought they were the coolest things ever. All through my teens I'd been holding on to the hope that one day I'd have a moment like that iconic ballroom scene in *A Cinderella Story*, where everyone would turn their heads and I'd feel beautiful and feel seen. And that happened for me at that photo shoot when I saw who I was through that lens for the first time.

You never know when that moment will come – and even if you don't want or need it, you might be surprised by how you feel when it happens. It doesn't have to be some big grand moment where people all turn their heads and look – it can be as simple as you seeing yourself the way someone else does.

MY FIRST SHOOT GAVE ME A TASTE FOR BEING THE PERSON AT THE CENTRE OF THE ACTION

the castle in the sky

As a little kid, I was always drawn to the most attractive person in a situation, whether they were on a screen, in a poster or at my school – they were like a magnet to me. I was obsessed with beauty. I'd see models in pictures and think, *Wow. Imagine being them. What would it feel like to be them?* To me, they belonged to a different world.

As I got older, I realised it wasn't just me who was drawn to attractive people – it was the whole world! The perception that good-looking people are more worthy than someone who isn't conventionally attractive is everywhere. It's a harmful and untrue perception, but it's one I felt on a deep level growing up.

It's kind of ironic that I'm a model now, because if you'd handed me a list of career options and said, 'Pick the job you're most likely to do as an adult', modelling would have been the last job I picked! For one thing, I always felt my Asian features were ugly, because that's the message I was given by the dominant culture as well as my own Filo culture. Whiter features were preferred – it was unsaid, but clear. But as I grew up and started embracing myself for who I actually was, rather than who I thought I needed to be, I realised the opposite was true. Now, my Asian features are the things I like MOST about my appearance. They're also the reason I get booked for certain jobs: they make me different. They make me stand out. They make me . . . me!

I think a lot of people experience similar 'full circle' moments, when a certain feature or character trait they once hated becomes the thing they like best about themselves. Everyone is looking for different things, so trying to be a version of one narrow beauty standard is a waste of time. You can never put your finger on what people find beautiful. Someone can be a supermodel, but that doesn't mean they're everyone's flavour.

These days, I see beauty as mostly coming from someone's heart and soul. You can meet a beautiful person, but if they have an ugly personality, your perception of their beauty changes and they're no longer beautiful to you. All you see is an ugly person. I've thought people were really attractive, and then been instantly turned off by things they've said or their attitude. And once that switch is flicked, there's no going back.

SOMEONE CAN BE A SUPERMODEL, BUT THAT DOESN'T MEAN THEY'RE EVERYONE'S FLAVOUR

To me, a great example of beauty is Zendaya. We love her because she's done so much with her life and she's vocal about many important issues. Yes, she's incredibly beautiful, but the things she stands for and the way she stands up for them make her beautiful on every level. As she ages, she'll still be that beautiful person because the essence of who she is will stay the same, or get even better.

Top: In my Lady Gaga wig!
Right: After I got blonde hair extensions.
Bottom: One of the final shots from the TFP uni project shoot.

MAJOR mood

online love

For some reason, I've never felt shy online, like I sometimes feel in real life. It feels natural and comfortable. I'd been posting videos for fun on YouTube since high school, but when I started transitioning, I had this overwhelming feeling of wanting to share my experiences and talk about my life in a real way.

On one level, this idea was scary, because it meant putting something so private into the world for anyone to see and comment on. But I couldn't stop thinking about how much I would have loved to see videos like that when I was younger – so it seemed worth the risk.

Once I decided to do social media, I wanted to use a different last name for my online presence – one that sounded like my real last name (Clemens), but was still different enough. Then I remembered that Blair had already given me the perfect name a couple of years earlier: Clementine. On our trips into the city, we'd always see this little store called Clementine's. It had such a cute vibe, and she'd always say, 'That's your shop! Wow! It's so French. You should run away to another country and call yourself Clementine!'

Blair was always dreaming up new adventures for us; she was always saying we should buy wigs, get new identities and run away to another country. She'd plan it all out and talk about how we were going to run away to New York and get an apartment together. I loved the way she dreamed big – it sparked that in me, too. It was like she was living in a movie. And I've kind of adopted that attitude for myself lately, because now my life does feel like a movie sometimes – only now I get to decide which role I'm playing. As a teen, I was strictly the side character. I had fun in that role, and it was right for that time in my life. But having certain friendships end pushed me to grow into a newer, bolder version of myself. I was ready to step into the lead role of my own spin-off show.

I feel so myself on social media that it's easy for me to express myself. It comes naturally, and I think people who interact with me feel that. I love the freedom and the whole creative process of filming and editing videos. When I started sharing my personal experiences online, it was amazing to see how many people were watching and liking those videos, becoming invested in my journey and – even better – relating to my experiences and finding strength in them. That was everything.

NOW I FELT READY TO STEP INTO THE LEAD ROLE OF MY OWN SPIN-OFF SHOW

But it's also been a lot to process, because having people on social media tell me they think I'm beautiful or companies wanting me to model for their campaigns has been a whole mindset shift for me. I never saw this life for myself. I was that little kid sneaking lip glosses to school for comfort, and now I have my own damn makeup palette. If that isn't life coming full circle, I don't know what is.

SHINE AND BE YOU, BBY

be YOUR first choice

The more comfortable you are in your skin, the easier it gets to be okay with yourself as you are – regardless of whether someone is choosing you first, second, or not at all. There will always be someone who's prettier, smarter and more talented than you are. That's true for everyone in the world – that's life! It doesn't mean you can't shine and be on the same level as they are.

the limit does
not exist

Gen Z has grown up in this weird time where we have access to all the information in the world online at our fingertips day and night – and the things we see create a lot of feelings. But we've also inherited a culture from older generations in which people aren't supposed to show any sign of struggle, keeping things bottled up and only showing the best versions of themselves online. So it's confusing for Gen Z to navigate/connect when things are so raw and real.

Gen Zs know that we are stronger when we show our vulnerabilities, when we show that we're human. We're trying to fight for that, but it's difficult when people in older generations tell us that we're too 'emotional', or that we don't understand the world as well as they do.

Even though I'm at the cusp of the transition between Gen Y and Gen Z and I'm an adult now, I still feel that type of judgement coming my way, and I've carried this insecurity into my working life. When I had an office job, I often felt I wasn't smart enough, especially when older people would say things like, 'Your brain is different to our brains because we didn't have social media growing up.' It would make me insecure, and I'd hate it.

Our experiences may be different, but life shouldn't be about inter-generational competitiveness or one-upmanship. No one needs to be saying, 'I'm the smarter one. You're clouded by all these other social media influences.' My generation has been shaped by social media, and maybe that does make us different, but why is that a negative thing? Maybe the old ways aren't working.

TikTok and other platforms aren't just about people dancing. There is so much information on those platforms – way more than any TV news show or newspaper could ever fit. There are also no boundaries, and you can't protect yourself from the things you might see and hear. You never know when you're going to come across something that pushes you over the edge. Young people absorb all this through their phones, and then carry it with them for the rest of their day. Some days, that's too much for one person to take.

HAVING A MORE CONNECTED WORLD CAN BE A DOOR TO THOSE 'SOMEDAY SOONS'

Social media isn't going anywhere. As scary as some may find that, having a more connected world may turn out to be the thing that saves some people. It can be a door to those 'someday soons' for people whose family or town is telling them that they don't fit, and that everything in life is black and white. Their phone will be right there in their hand showing them that this is NOT true – showing them how many different types of people there are in the world, how many places there are to see, how many experiences they can have. The world is a rainbow, and there are no limits to who someone can be, who they can love or where they can go.

let's cry together

When my older brother Dane got engaged to his girlfriend, KC, and they asked me to be one of their bridesmaids, dreams I didn't even know I had started to come true. Thanks to the pandemic, I ended up having a whole extra year to process the fact that I'd be seeing my biological dad and my half-sister, Kali, for the first time in ten years. I was so nervous about reconnecting, but I'd also come such a long way from the confused child – and, later, the angry, resentful teen – who'd pushed my dad away. I was in a happier place, more mature, and ready to move on from the past. To limit the awkwardness at the wedding, I decided to reach out to both of them a few days beforehand, and those few casual messages broke the ice.

such a special moment

When Kali and I saw each other, we just clicked – that sister bond was still there. Within minutes, we were making jokes and sharing moments, and it wasn't long before we both broke down crying, too, because we'd missed out on so much of each other's lives. All this time, I thought maybe she hated me or thought I was a bad sister, but there was no hate. When I made a speech at the wedding about how grateful I was for my big brother, how I'd always appreciated his protection and unconditional love, and how much fun we'd had growing up, I looked over and saw that Kali was crying.

Later that night, she told me that she'd always felt left out when it came to all of us. She'd grown up feeling like an only child, even though she had siblings. That really hit me hard and made me so sad. We'd wasted so much time. We'd always had a good relationship as kids; the only thing that had separated us was my feeling of uncertainty. I didn't know how to be an older sister to Kali. It was never about Kali. And since her family didn't exactly see eye to eye with my mum (families can be like that), we had this whole other layer of tension floating around. Living in different states only made it harder to stay connected.

My biological dad was still the same quiet, chilled man. He still liked surfing and fishing, and he liked Ryan. He didn't hold anything against me for rejecting his attempts at reconnecting, or ignoring his invitations to visit. The love and acceptance had always been there. He told me he wished he'd been a bigger part of my life, and that he would have liked to have supported my transition more. He said I always had him if I needed him. And that meant so much to me. I really felt that fatherly vibe from him that I'd been missing.

I REALISED THE LOVE AND ACCEPTANCE HAD ALWAYS BEEN THERE

When Kali shared her thoughts about my journey later that weekend, I couldn't believe how woke she was. My head was spinning as I listened to her talk about LGBTQ+ and trans issues. I was thinking, *Wow! She's using all the right words and terms, effortlessly. She did care!* I could tell she'd been talking about these issues with people for a while, and that it wasn't just for show. It turned out that whenever my biological dad had struggled to understand trans issues, Kali was the one educating him about it, breaking things down for him

Above: Having a moment
in my bridesmaid dress.
Left: With the happy couple.
Bottom: With Kali on her
twenty-first birthday.

SiSTERS
ReuNiTed!

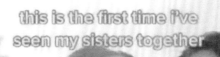

this is the first time i've seen my sisters together

feeling the love

Top: The TikTok I made about our reunion went viral.
Bottom: Dane, me and Kali with our biological dad.

so he could understand. She'd taken on that role, even though I'd left her fully out of my life. It made me so sad that I'd blocked that connection and cut myself off from their support.

That reunion made me reflect on how I'd felt as a child. How a simple interaction – like taking a toy from a child, or making them feel like they're doing something wrong – can warp a child's perception of a person or a situation for a long time. When children are little, they see the adults in their life and think, *Wow, I want to be like them!* But a negative experience can switch that thinking to, *I don't feel good here.* Kali's mum hadn't been out to hurt me, she just hadn't understood me.

Finding out that we were all good, and that there was love there, lifted a million weights off my shoulders. We're starting the next chapter fresh.

Seeing KC walk up the aisle to my brother was such a stunning princess moment. I felt this rush of happiness – for her, for my brother, for all of us. I looked over at my younger sister, Kiki, standing next to Kali – I'd never seen them together before that day – and they were both in tears. All three of us were. My biological dad had tears in his eyes, too. It was a beautiful fairytale moment. There were no words spoken, but we were all joined, and there was nothing but acceptance and love.

and at last
I see the light

If you've reached these last pages and you're looking for my 'recipe for success' or my 'top ten tips for transitioning' – they aren't here, bby! Life is too messy and complicated for that – but it's also better and more surprising than you can imagine. All I can show you is my life. Everything I've shared in these pages is a real experience I've lived through. I haven't sugar-coated anything or tried to make situations into something they're not. I've simply laid them out for you – as I remember them – in the hope that you can take whatever you need from them right now.

out-of-body experience)

At the cover shoot for this book you're holding, there was so much positivity in the room. I was sitting against a background of baby-blue tulle, and Johnny the photographer was showing me the stills, saying, 'These are looking so good!' I was looking at them, and listening to his words, but suddenly I had this sense of things not being real – of me not being real. It was too much, and I started crying uncontrollably. Everyone around me was shocked, and my managers, Sim and Sarah, ran over to see what had happened. But I couldn't put it into words. How do you explain how it feels to be in a dream you thought was untouchable?

I'd been talking about this book for so long. We'd been planning it. I was deep in the writing process and I'd been going through the motions at the shoot. It wasn't until that exact moment that the weight of this landed on me. It became real to me that someone out there – a young girl or boy – might pick this up, read my words and find something in them to hold on to. One of my stories might lift them up and push them forward when they need it. I would have done anything for that – not only to have had a book like this, but also to have had a face I could relate to. It means everything to be that for someone else.

I looked around at all the talented people in that room and felt the positive energy and passion they were bringing to this project. Each one of them was there to support me, and that made me feel like I had an army behind me. Another family. You'll be surprised where you find family in life. It doesn't have to be within the four walls you grow up in.

YOU DESERVE THE GOOD THING THAT IS HAPPENING TO YOU. IT IS REAL. IT IS TRULY YOURS

When a landmark moment appears in your life, know that it is okay for you to grab it and feel it. Know that you deserve the good thing that is happening to you. It IS real. It is yours and it is truly something that you deserve. Everything I'd been working on had been leading me to this moment – every tear, every laugh, every heartbreak stored within these pages. And even though I was crying, I wasn't sad. (I mean, I do cry about everything, but this time the tears were happy ones.)

Ryan and Bambi were waiting for me after the shoot wrapped. They'd planned this whole fun afternoon out for us and were all excited to hear how the shoot had gone. When I told them that I'd broken down, they were instantly so sympathetic, and asked if I wanted to cancel our plans, but I said, 'NO! I feel energised!' I had so much adrenaline. I felt powerful and ready to take on the world.

A STORY I ONCE BELIEVED WOULD NOT BE HEARD OR UNDERSTOOD WAS FINALLY BEING BROUGHT INTO THE SPOTLIGHT

This was unlike any feeling I'd ever had at a shoot. I've modelled for several brand campaigns over the past few years, and as much as I love seeing companies doing the work to represent the LGBTQ+ community in positive and high-profile ways, those jobs are still work. When I show up on set, I'm there to do my job, support the brand and get through their shot list. At the end of the day, it means more visibility for trans people, and I'm all about that – but I'm there to promote that brand's message. And no matter how positive that message is, it's still their take on things.

That's what hit different at this photo shoot. This time, the message was 100 per cent my own. A message and story I once believed would not be heard or understood by the world was being brought into the spotlight. I'd transcended limitations put on me by the world, and by myself, and I wasn't done yet. I was just getting started.

Alice, Bambi, Grace and me at my Disney princess–inspired birthday party.

kid, you'll move mountains

Ultimately, I'm out here in the spotlight because I want ALL of us to transcend our current situations and expectations. I want trans people to be treated equally. I want people who spread hate to find empathy and open their minds. I'm doing what I can to be visible and vocal, but it's a lot of pressure, and it gets heavy some days. Many of my trans sisters and brothers are doing similar things – they're shining in their own corners of the internet and moving things forward by sharing their experiences. But it's heavy for them, too – scroll through any one of their comments sections and you'll see that. We're doing what we can, but we're fighting an entire transphobic culture one post and one comment at a time. We need back-up.

A lot comes down to media. The way our stories are told – if they're told at all – matters. Those things are shaping kids right now, the same way they shaped me. When a trans woman is murdered, the story isn't reported in the same way as a cis white woman's murder. There's not the same energy around it – the subtext is loaded, and it's not given the same weight as the other stories, even though both stories are equally important.

There's so much I want to see changed. I want trans people to be normalised and respected. I want society to reach a point where there's enough education and understanding about trans people that the violence, murder and suicide rates that plague our community start coming down. I want to see more compassion and support for trans kids, and more protection for trans people. It's about human rights at this point.

Right now, as you're reading this, there are trans kids who are starting their journey. I'd like to say that things are changing fast enough for them, but I can't. The truth is, I don't think enough is being done. I can't say that those kids won't be bullied at school, judged by their teachers or struggle to find jobs when they grow up. As much as there are great steps being made, with major brands giving more visibility to LGBTQ+ people, life in the real world tells a different story.

RIGHT NOW, AS YOU'RE READING THIS, TRANS KIDS ARE STARTING THEIR JOURNEY

Just the other night, Ryan and I went for Korean barbecue at a busy restaurant in the city. There was a group of businessmen having dinner behind us. They were speaking loudly, and at one point, they started talking about pronouns, and how they shouldn't have to worry about using certain pronouns when they emailed a particular person at work. One of the men said – LOUDLY – 'If it has a dick, it's a dude, and if it has a vag, it's a female.' And all six men at the table laughed.

I wasn't shocked that he thought that, but I was confused by the fact that he felt so comfortable making that comment loudly and with a sense of . . . pride. There was no hint of, *Hmm, this might be a bad thing to say. Maybe I should lower my voice or not say it at all.*

If anything, he said it loudly enough that other diners would hear. Maybe he thought they'd smile and think, *Yeah, bro! We agree.* He said it knowing he wouldn't be called out, and he was right. Not one person at that table said or did anything to counter his viewpoint. And as much as I wanted to say something in the moment, I knew it wasn't a safe or smart thing for me to do.

The world may be changing on the surface, but we know how it is behind the scenes. A person might say, 'Sure, I'll respect your pronouns.' But often times there isn't respect, and people don't take us seriously. They don't give slurs or throwaway comments a second thought, or see how comments like those breed a culture of hate. Some of the men at that table might be fathers, and those jokes and attitudes will trickle down to their kids, then get spread through schoolyards. And vulnerable kids will suffer because of it.

THERE'S WORK TO DO, AND IT NEEDS TO BE DONE EVERY DAY. IT LITERALLY STARTS WITH ALL OF US

More needs to be done to wake people up. Minds can be changed when someone comes across a story that alters their perception, or when they meet someone in the trans community. But it shouldn't take having a trans kid or meeting a trans person to make people realise that trans people are human, too. It shouldn't be so hard for people to show kindness.

There's work to do, and it needs to be done every day. It literally starts with all of us. We have so much more power than we realise. When you come across something hateful or hear something you don't agree with – action can be as simple as not giving any reaction at all. Silence speaks loudly. Or, if you feel safe pointing out that what they're saying is harmful or wrong, do that. Or say, 'That's not funny.' It might not sound like much, but don't underestimate how much of an effect it can have. Not getting approval stings, and the person you're calling out may be salty in the moment, but they may also go away and reflect: *Okay. Why didn't he laugh?* Or *Why did she say it wasn't funny?*

Sometimes, a person's way of thinking will be so ingrained that this won't be enough to make them rethink their behaviour. But that doesn't mean we shouldn't try, every chance we get. If we aren't paying attention to moments where we feel we have a voice to be used, then nothing is going to change. We can't just hope things will get better after our generation. We can't wait another ten or twenty years for that to happen. And we can't make anything better if we let toxic people speak for us or belittle our voices.

LIFE CAN BE A DREAM,
BUT IT ISN'T A FAIRYTALE.
THERE'S NO FAIRY GODMOTHER.
NO MAGIC SWORD.
NO KNIGHT IN SHINING ARMOUR.
WE HAVE TO BE THOSE
THINGS FOR OURSELVES.

BUT THAT IS MORE THAN POSSIBLE.
HEROES SURVIVE USING WHAT'S ALREADY
INSIDE OF THEM. IT'S NOT MAGIC OR
BEAUTY THAT WINS THE DAY, IT'S COURAGE,
KINDNESS AND COMPASSION. THESE ARE
THE THINGS THAT MOVE MAIN CHARACTERS
TO THE NEXT PART OF THEIR STORY.
HANDSOME PRINCES AND FAIRY GODMOTHERS
ARE NICE, BUT THEY'RE JUST WINDOW
DRESSING. AND THEY'RE NOTHING
COMPARED TO YOU.

love always,
AJ xo

LEAN ON ME

These days, there's more support than ever out there for people in the LGBTQ+ community and their allies. There are places you can turn to for real help, so please don't ever struggle on alone. The helplines and resources listed here are just a start. Remember, you are loved!

Australia

♥ **QLife** provides free, anonymous LGBTQ+ support and referrals for people wanting to talk about sexuality, identity, gender, bodies, feelings or relationships. Call **1800 184 527** for a phone chat – or to webchat, go to **qlife.org.au/**.

♥ **Kids Helpline** provides phone counselling and crisis support to kids, teens and young adults, plus heaps of online resources for youths, parents and carers. Call **1800 55 1800**.

♥ **Lifeline** is a 24-hour crisis support and suicide prevention helpline, available Australia-wide, for anyone experiencing a personal crisis. Call **13 11 14**.

♥ **MINUS18** offers support and fun, safe events for LGBTQ+ young people, and also runs school workshops and workplace training to build social inclusion and tackle discrimination. Go to **minus18.org.au**.

♥ **ReachOut.com** has links to all sorts of LGBTQ+ support services for young people, parents and schools. Go to **au.reachout.com/**.

♥ **The Equality Project** provides information to support LGBTQ+ inclusion and human rights. More info at **theequalityproject.org.au/policy**.

New Zealand

♥ **OUTLine** has a free, confidential, nationwide support line for the rainbow community, their friends, whānau, and those questioning. Speak to trained LGBTQ+ volunteers from 6 pm to 9 pm on **0800 688 5463**, and find further resources for parents and workplaces at **outline.org.nz**.

♥ **RainbowYOUTH** can put queer, gender diverse, takatāpui and intersex youth in touch with lots of support services, and offers info and resources for parents and teachers. See **ry.org.nz**.

♥ **InsideOUT** at **insideout.org.nz** also lists lots of places where you can get support.

♥ **Skylight** has links to a wide range of resources for LGBTQ+ youth (and their families and allies), including counselling and support services, at **skylight.org.nz**. For info on counselling, call **0800 299 100**.

United Kingdom

♥ **Switchboard LGBT+ helpline** is run by LGBTQ+ volunteers to help you with whatever you want to talk about, including sexuality, gender identity, sexual health and emotional well-being. Open 10 am to 10 pm every day, call **0300 330 0630**.

♥ Text **SHOUT** to **85258** for free 24/7 help with anxiety, depression, suicidal thoughts, relationship problems, bullying or feeling overwhelmed. Text service available from all major mobile networks in the UK.

♥ The **Stonewall** and **Stonewall Youth** organisations provide information and support for LGBTQ+ communities and their allies, including links to resources, counselling referrals and emergency hotlines. Go to **stonewall.org.uk** and **youngstonewall.org.uk**, or freephone **0800 0502020** Monday to Friday, 9.30 am to 4.30 pm.

♥ **The Proud Trust** offers help and heaps of networks and resources for LGBTQ+ youth, including links to emergency helplines (click on 'Don't Suffer in Silence'), at **theproudtrust.org**.

United States

♥ **The Trevor Project** has LGBTQ+ counsellors 24/7 for young people who are in crisis, feeling suicidal, or need a safe space to talk – call the TrevorLifeline on **1 866 488 7386**. For their confidential text message service, text **START** to **678 678**. For an online chat service, go to **thetrevorproject.org** – where you'll also find links to all kinds of helpful resources.

♥ **Stonewall Youth** has programs run by and for LGBTQ+ youth. Go to **stonewallyouth.org**.

♥ The **Centers for Disease Control and Prevention (CDC)** has a wide range of resources for LGBTQ+ youth, their friends, educators, parents and family. See **cdc. gov/lgbthealth/youth-resources.htm**.

♥ **GLAAD** is an LGBTQ+ rights organisation, at **glaad.org**.

T H a N K F u L

The magic within these pages would not be complete
without these angels, so I would like to thank them . . .

First, without their guidance and encouragement,
I would be so lost, so thank you Sarah Etinger and Simone
Reginato for believing in me. For not only being fabulous
agents but also truly feeling like family to me.

Second, the wonderful Katie Bosher, you have been
a dream to co-write with and without the essence you
brought to the book, none of this would have been real.
You helped shape my experiences within these pages
and I'm forever grateful.

Third, Lou Johnson for taking a chance on me to
create this book, for caring about my story and being
passionate about it, for pitching my idea to Murdoch Books
and making this happen. And certainly the same love for
Ruby, for following my story and sharing it with Lou.

Fourth, the true beauty behind the images for this
book, Johnny Diaz Nicolaidis, an extremely talented
photographer; the wonderful Tory Price for bringing my

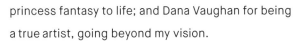

I LOVE YOU ANGELS!

princess fantasy to life; and Dana Vaughan for being a true artist, going beyond my vision.

Fifth, Ryan (partner) and Bambi (best friend) for holding my hand through it all, being true friends, family and basically everything I've searched for throughout my life. Your love inspires me and I adore you both.

Sixth, my family for your acceptance and unconditional love. Of course to my mother, Anilyn Esteban, for showing me true courage and kindness in a world that can sometimes go against you.

Seventh, the Murdoch Books team, everyone who has brought life, charm and meaning to the book. Thank you to each and every one of you.

Lastly, the incredible people in my life who inspired the stories and celebrated my achievements – Aunty Zeny, Roxy, Kuya Dane, Kali, Kiki, the beautiful supportive community I'm so lucky to have, and the beat-up blonde Lady Gaga wig.

Published in 2021 by Murdoch Books,
an imprint of Allen & Unwin

Murdoch Books Australia
83 Alexander Street
Crows Nest NSW 2065
Phone: +61 (0)2 8425 0100
murdochbooks.com.au
info@murdochbooks.com.au

Murdoch Books UK
Ormond House
26–27 Boswell Street
London WC1N 3JZ
Phone: +44 (0) 20 8785 5995
murdochbooks.co.uk
info@murdochbooks.co.uk

For corporate orders and custom publishing,
contact our business development team at
salesenquiries@murdochbooks.com.au.

Publisher: Lou Johnson
Co-writer: Katie Bosher
Editorial Manager: Julie Mazur Tribe
Design Manager: Megan Pigott
Designer: Madeleine Kane
Editor: Katri Hilden
Production Director: Lou Playfair

Definition of 'transcend' on p. 5 adapted
from *Macquarie Dictionary*.

List of book recommendations on p. 37 written
by Paul Emerich France. Originally published
31 May 2019 on Edutopia.org.

ISBN 978 1 92235 160 9 Australia
ISBN 978 1 91166 837 4 UK

 A catalogue record for this
book is available from the
National Library of Australia

A catalogue record for this book is available
from the British Library

Colour reproduction by Splitting Image
Colour Studio Pty Ltd, Clayton, Victoria
Printed by C&C Offset Printing Co. Ltd., China

10 9 8 7 6 5 4 3 2 1

MIX
Paper from
responsible sources
FSC® C008047